The Secrets Decoded

The Science of Prosperity, Success, Wealth, Health and Happiness.

Edited and Written By:

George S. Mentz, JD, MBA, CWM

With selected content from:

Thomas Troward
Wallace Wattles
Charles Haanel
James Allen
Christian Larson
William Walker Atkinson
Ralph Waldo Emerson

"Enter the 4th Dimension, reach up, reach out and expand your mind."

Executive Summaries on the teachings of: Wattles, Haanel, Troward, James Allen, Think and Grow Rich, Metaphysics, Atkinson, Christian Larson and much much more

ISBN 9780615159621

George Mentz, JD, MBA

Printed in the United States of America

ISBN 9780615159621

ISBN 978-0-6151-5962-1

90000

ID: 1106213
www.lulu.com

9 780615 159621

978-0-6151-5926-1   (90000)

For more information, tools, free books and other information see:
www.mastersofthesecrets.com
www.secretdecoded.com

The Secrets Decoded

Table of Contents

George Mentz, JD, MBA

Dedication:

This book is dedicated to : Wallace Wattles, Thomas Troward, Charles Haanel, Joseph Murphy, Robert Collier, James Allen, Napoleon Hill, Prentice Mulford, Ralph Waldo Emerson, and the growing community of Self Improvement, New Thought, Mind Sciences, Higher Thought, and Mental Science.

Summary:

This advanced executive analysis of the Masters of the Secrets is like a combined gospel of the laws of attraction, laws of increase, laws of gratitude, and laws of action, health & success. If you want wealth, health, and peace of mind, this book is a masterpiece and collection of insights from the greats. Advanced strategies based on: The Science of Getting Rich, The Edinburgh Lectures, Think and Grow Rich, The Master Key System, Thomas Troward, Charles Haanel or Wallace Wattles, James Allen, Teachings of the Original Book by Napoleon Hill, Christian Larson, Teachings of Joseph Murphy, and more.

This book has several exciting features: Commentary on the following authors and books is included: Wallace Wattles, Dr. Joseph Murphy, Judge Thomas Troward, Dr. Emerson, Dr. Charles Haanel, Dr. Christian Larson, Dr. Napoleon Hill, Prentice Mulford, The Master Key System, and Robert Collier. This book also contains an inspiring version of: The 8 Fold Path, 25 Secrets to Gratitude, a metaphysical Exercise for Health by Wattles, 12 Steps for Abundance, and an prosperity analysis of the Beatitudes.

You Are Chosen

What every your race, believe that it is good and great. Whatever your education, believe that you can be better as more knowledge and understanding of the laws of life are needed. Regardless of your appearances, you can look better, improve yourself, be healthy, and enhance your image in your unique way. It does not matter what religion you belong, your spiritual knowledge and awareness can be cultivated to a new dimension where peace of mind is yours.

You are a Genius. You have been chosen to do great things and live a significant life. You have talent from the universe. You must allow your assets and skills to be honed and sharpened. Do not die with your vision and talents unused. You are special, and you can be whatever you want within your sphere of availability and grow accordingly toward your destiny.

There is nothing wrong with being confident in who you are. Only good can come from growth. Sometimes change is difficult, but the re-invention or rebirth of your true self is available NOW.

The essays and passages in this book should be read carefully and you will be empowered with this information. If this is new to you, that is fine. Keep an open mind, learn the metaphysical insights in this book, and allow yourself to reach the great heights that you are meant to achieve.

Spiritual Mind-Set & Mental Attitude

You remember the saying of the sacred writer: "As a man thinketh in his heart, so is he." A truer statement never was uttered. For everyman or woman is what he or she is, by reason of what he or she has thought. We have thought ourselves into what we are. One's place in life is largely determined by their mental attitude, constructive thinking, forces of gratitude, and being contemplative in action.

In the sense in which I use the term, "Constructive or Positive" means Confident expectation, Self-Confidence, Courage, Initiative, Energy, Optimism, and Expectation of good.

As a matter of fact, the great scientific authorities of the present time distinctly teach that a man by diligent care and practice may completely change his character, temperament, and habits. He may kill out undesirable traits of character, and replace them by new and desirable traits, qualities and faculties. This is sometimes why many people refer to themselves to being: reinvented, in harmony, connected, reborn, or have greater peace of mind.

The brain is now known to be the instrument and tool of something called Mind, which uses the brain as its instrument of expression. Did you ever stop long enough to think that we are constantly giving other people suggestive impressions of ourselves and qualities? Do you not know that, if you go about with the Mental Attitude of Discouragement, Fear, Lack of Self-Confidence, and all the other Negative qualities of mind, other people are sure to catch the impression and govern themselves toward you accordingly? Do you know people who have the destructive"I Can't Mentality?" Are you not affected by their manifested Mental Attitude? And further, these mind sets are the result of the constant daily thought of these men and their Mental Attitude internally and projected externally toward their environment.

The method of the action of Mental Attitude towards Spiritual and Financial Abundance may be called the working of the Law of Attraction. Now without attempting to advance any wild theories, I must assert that all thinking, observing men have noticed the operation of a mental Law of Attraction, whereby "like attracts like." A person's Mental Attitude acts as a magnet, attracting the things, objects, circumstances, environments, and people in harmony with that Mental Status and Attitude. Fix your mind firmly upon anything, good or bad, in the world, and you attract it to you or are attracted to it in obedience to the LAW. You attract to you the things you expect, what you think about, what you are willing to have, and to whatever you direct and focus in your Mental Energy.

The person who thinks, talks, and expects wealth and prosperity attracts, or is attracted to, people of wealth and comes, in time to share their prosperity with them. Sweep out from the chambers of your mind all these miserable negative thoughts like "I can't," "That's just my luck," "I knew I'd do it," "I don't deserve it", "Success and Abundance is Bad", "Poor me," etc., and fill up the mind with the strong, constructive, positive, invigorating, helpful, forceful, compelling thinking and ideals such as: Success, Confidence, Health, Peace of Mind, and Expectation of that which you desire. And, just as the steel fillings fly to the attraction of the magnet, so will that which you need fly to you in response to this great natural principle of mental action - the Law of Attraction. Begin this very moment and build up a new a new character of thinking and ideal - that of Peace, Health, Financial Success and Abundance. See it mentally - expect it - demand it! This is the way to create it in your Enhanced Spiritual & Mental Attitude of Prosperity.

Think and Grow Rich – Philosophy of Dr. Napoleon Hill

The original book by Napoleon Hill was based on interviews with hundreds of America's greatest business executives and political leaders. The manuscript took about twenty years to complete. As stated in the original, great ventures begin with an idea. Ideas are thoughts. Thoughts can turn into real things. What stimulates thought? Desire. Strong desires are the basis and beginning of most successes. A strong desire is usually what can bring an idea into a reality. Take your desire and hone it. Cultivate a plan and refine it. Read it daily and you will begin to self-actualize the concepts and apply the actions necessary in your daily life to move in the direction of your dreams. Napoleon Hill places much emphasis on attitude, or constructive thinking. This constructive attitude and thinking transmutes into faith. Based on his research with the most successful executives, Hill believed that belief and faith are the major forces that--when coupled with desire--can propel a plan into success. He equated faith with constructive belief and effective life force.

Planning is also crucial because most people do not define what they will do or how they will do it in any degree of specificity. Thus, he refers to having a <u>definite purpose</u>. This simply means to seize upon a specific goal or quest. <u>Be very specific</u>. Write it down, hone it, and do it. He also places much weight on education, skill improvement, and continuous learning in relation to your goals.

Firmly establish what you want and write it out in specific terms:

- State what you want to accomplish (the dollar amount or specific thing or attribute).
- State what you will give to earn the outcome (effort, work, etc.).
- Write the date it will happen.
- Sign and date the plan.
- Read the plan daily upon awakening and before going to sleep.
- Feel you have it now in heart and mind.

Strategic Characteristics of Your Plans and Actions

> ➤ Your actions must be persistent, effective, and efficient.
> ➤ Your decisions must be strong and unwavering.
> ➤ You must not procrastinate and you must make and act on healthy decisions.
> ➤ Strong thoughts of belief and faith will bring about change in the future, yourself, and the environment. Feel in your heart and see in your mind that you have the thing right now. Feel the emotion of having it, and give thanks for receiving it.

As for your character, write out another list:

> ➤ Write a description of who you want to become.
> ➤ Formulate a written plan detailing how you will achieve it.
> ➤ Desire, thought, and action will gradually transform your character improvement into reality.
> ➤ Self-confidence can be built on affirmations, gratitude, and faith.
> ➤ Eliminate destructive thinking and negative attitude through harmonious thinking and harmlessness In your actions. Example: Engage win-win relationships.
> ➤ Do what you need to do to improve your mind, body, and soul on a daily basis.

As for the process of meditation, autosuggestion, or affirmations create another list:

> ➤ Find a quiet spot to relax.
> ➤ Read your written statements of desire.
> ➤ Believe in your mind that the outcome will occur.
> ➤ See that you have it already in your mind's eye.
> ➤ Believe that you can and will receive it.
> ➤ Put the statement out where you can see it easily.
> ➤ As such, the only limits to your goals are your state of mind and faith.

Discuss your goals with other professionals who want to help you. This is known as the Master Mind Alliance. We suggests that you team up with other professionals with related goals and expertise to obtain counsel. In this alliance, you give as much as you receive in a harmonious fashion while always supporting the group members with your insight, advice, and help.

Overall, a definiteness of purpose of your plan along with a burning desire is generally what is needed to accomplish great things. When you mix this recipe with constructive belief or faith, you become driven to do what is necessary to succeed and *not* to give up. You believe that *you can.*

A burning desire is something that you really want to do. You are solid in your faith that you can allow your desire to become real. You are willing to sever the past and move forward with the desire, goal, and plan. You are willing to focus exclusively on the project, and never give up. You are guaranteed degrees of success if you do something each day toward the completion of your goals.

You develop a state of mind that is conducive to your desires. You have positive thoughts, enthusiasm, belief, and persistence that are all built on truth. Truth can be perceived in a constructive way or in the form of doom and gloom. We all know that a bitter and negative attitude is not an effective way to live and can actually paralyze you, resulting in failure. As they say, "Realists expect failure and demand to be right." Seeing beyond what is apparent takes skill and practice. When exercising the principles of Napoleon Hill in your life, you will obtain this skill over time.

Do you have trouble with constructive belief? Napoleon Hill wrote about methods in his book that are timeless and were heavily used in the self-help movement in the early 1900's. See other authors: Thomas Troward, Wallace Wattles, Christian Larson, W. Atkinson, and more. As stated by many of these masters of self-help, constructive belief and expectation can be cultivated and transformed into a great asset and strength, which will lead to greater success.

Faith can be induced through several practices or exercises:

- Mental images of success. Picture yourself completing your goals in detail.
- Affirmations (reading aloud the attributes or goals that you desire). This can be applied to your character, family, or business dreams. Example: "I am the best teacher, manager, professional etc." or "I am getting better and better every day."
- Gratitude and thankfulness of heart. Think deeply over the gifts of life that you have received on a daily basis. Cultivate a thankful heart based on what you already have or what you will have. Examples: Home, family, health, and more.
- Remember: Like attracts like. Therefore, attitude and character development are about attracting the greater good. Thus, thankfulness and praise are key to attracting higher good.

Building a Master Mind Alliance Network Tips:

- Develop friends who can give you insight and support who will not fill your mind with doubt or thoughts of failure.
- You should be willing to help all in this group of friends with your insight, skill, and support.
- Meet often for planning.
- You must always speak and act in an encouraging way to maintain harmony.
- Know each day what you will do to move forward with your plans.
- Avoid lack of decision and procrastination, and stick with your decisions.
- Continue to organize, adapt, and strive to succeed.

As for life energy, Napoleon Hill implies that we have many forms of energy. These include our forces of attraction or sexual energy. Thus, concentration is critical to focus all forms of your life energy toward your desires. As you know, if you are focusing your primary energies in several areas, you are, in essence, distracted. To prevent distraction, transmute your: mental, Spiritual, physical, and attraction/sexual energies toward your dreams.

You must detach from too-rigid expectations and flow with life. Be specific in your goals, but be open to something better or a little different to come to you as a result of your working of these methods. Additionally, you must also condition the mind to cooperate with the direction that your want to go by cultivating constructive thinking and action. Thus, do not allow yourself to destroy your self-confidence with fear or self-sabotage. Your new constructive belief, faith, desire, and enthusiasm will carry through to the finish line. You will transcend your old thinking into a higher thought.

Your subconscious mind can be influenced through your actions. Therefore, project the image of success onto the "picture screen" of subconscious mind, using a heartfelt energy. Heartfelt energy is emotional thinking that is tied to your mental picture of success.

Therefore, your constructive belief, thankful heart, desires, planning and alliances will allow you to lead a more harmonious relationship with the universal forces. Your gratitude, constructive expectation, and efficient action will bring you in tune with universal forces and allow you to develop peace of mind and effective actions. Your harmonious Spiritual and physical actions will induce your mind and the world to cooperate with you and others will be attracted to help you.

In sum, the Universal Spirit will send you ideas and people to cooperate with you. In sum, the world will create opportunity for you and assist you with your dreams. Napoleon Hill alludes to all of this as the "sixth sense." Through the aid of the sixth sense, you may seek out certain goals, and they may not materialize. However, if you continue your work and constructive expectation, something better will come to you at the right time. Therefore, the Universe or sixth sense will protect you and assist your decision-making process.

The Mind Philosophy of Dr. Christian D. Larson

* Larson's writings have inspired the establishment of several movements, books, and even religions

To use the power of the mind, the first essential is to direct every mental action toward the goal in view, and this direction must not be occasional, but constant. Most minds, however, do not apply this law. They think about a certain thing one moment, and about something else the next moment. At a certain hour their mental actions work along a certain line, and at the next hour those actions work along a different line. Sometimes the goal in view is one thing, and sometimes another, so the actions of the mind do not move constantly toward a certain definite goal, but are mostly scattered. We know, however, that individuals who are actually working themselves steadily and surely toward the goal they have in view, invariably direct all the power of their thought upon that goal. In their mind not a single mental action is thrown away, not a single mental force wasted. All the power that is in them is being directed to work for what they wish to accomplish, and the reason that every power responds in this way is because they are not thinking of one thing now and something else the next moment.

The second essential is to make every mental action positive. When we desire certain things or when we think of certain things we wish to attain or achieve, the question should be if our mental attitudes at the time are positive or negative. To answer this we only have to remember that every positive action always goes toward that which receives its attention, whereas a negative action always retreats. A positive action is an action that you feel when you realize that every force in your entire system is pushed forward, so to speak, and that it is passing through what may be termed an expanding and enlarging state of feeling or consciousness.

The principle is to direct the power of mind upon the very highest, the very largest, and the very greatest mental conception of that which we intend to achieve. The first essential, therefore, is to direct the full power of mind and thought upon the goal in view, and to continue to direct the mind in that manner every minute, regardless of circumstances or conditions. The second essential is to make every mental action positive.

The third essential in the right use of the mind is to make every mental action constructive. A constructive mental action is one that is based upon a deep-seated desire to develop, to increase, to achieve, to attain--in brief, to become larger and greater, and to do something of far greater worth than has been done before. If you will cause every mental action you entertain to have that feeling, constructiveness will soon became second nature to your entire mental system; that is, all the forces of your mind will begin to become building forces, and will continue to build you up along any line through which you may desire to act.

Inspire your mind constantly with a building desire, and make this desire so strong that every part of your system will constantly feel that it wants to become greater, more capable and more efficient. An excellent practice in this connection is to try to enlarge upon all your ideas of things whenever you have spare moments for real thought. This practice will tend to produce a growing tendency in every process of your thinking. Another good practice is to inspire every mental action with more ambition. We cannot have too much ambition. We may have too much aimless ambition, but we cannot have too much real constructive ambition. If your ambition is very strong, and is directed toward something definite, every action of your mind, every action of your personality, and every action of your faculties will become constructive; that is, all those actions will be inspired by the tremendous force of your ambition to work for the realization of that ambition.

Never permit restless ambition. Whenever you feel the force of ambition, direct your mind at once in a calm, determined manner upon that which you really want to accomplish in life. Make this a daily practice, and you will steadily train all your faculties and powers not only to work for the realization of that ambition, but become more and more efficient in that direction. Before long your forces and faculties will be sufficiently competent to accomplish what you want.

In the proper use of the mind therefore, these three essentials should be applied constantly and thoroughly. First, direct all the powers of mind, all the powers of thought, and all your thinking upon the goal you have in view. Second, train every mental action to be deeply and calmly positive. Third, train every mental action to be constructive, to be filled with a building Spirit, to be inspired with a ceaseless desire to develop the greater, to achieve the greater, to attain the greater. When you have acquired these three, you will begin to use your forces in such a way that results must follow. You will begin to move forward steadily and surely, and you will be constantly gaining ground. Your mind will have become like the stream mentioned above. It will gather volume and force as it moves on and on, until finally that volume will be great enough to remove any obstacle in its way, and that force powerful enough to do anything you may have in view.

In order to apply these three essentials in the most effective manner, there are several misuses of the mind that must be avoided. Avoid the forceful, the aggressive, and the domineering attitudes, and do not permit your mind to become intense, unless it is under perfect control. Never attempt to control or influence others in any way whatever. You will seldom succeed in that manner, and when you do, the success will be temporary; besides, such a practice always weakens your mind.

Do not turn the power of your mind upon others, but turn it upon yourself in such a way that it will make you stronger, more positive, more capable, and more efficient. As you develop in this manner, success must come of itself. There is only one way you can influence others legitimately and that is through the giving of instruction, but in that case, there is no desire to influence. You desire simply to impart knowledge and information, and you exercise a most desirable influence without desiring to do so.

A great many men and women, after discovering the immense power of mind, have come to the conclusion that they might change circumstances by exercising mental power upon those circumstances in some mysterious manner, but such a practice means nothing but a waste of energy.

The way to control circumstances is to control the forces within yourself to make a greater human being of yourself, and as you become greater and more competent, you will naturally gravitate into better circumstances. In this connection, we should remember that like attracts like. If you want that which is better, make yourself better. If you want to realize the ideal, make yourself more ideal. If you want better friends, make yourself a better friend. If you want to associate with people of worth, make yourself more worthy. If you want to meet that which is agreeable, make yourself more agreeable. If you want to enter conditions and circumstances that are more pleasing, make yourself more pleasing. In brief, whatever you want, produce that something in yourself, and you will positively gravitate towards the corresponding conditions in the external world.

But to improve yourself along those lines, it is necessary to apply for that purpose all the power you possess. You cannot afford to waste any of it, and every misuse of the mind will waste power. Avoid all destructive attitudes of the mind, such an anger, hatred, malice, envy, jealousy, revenge, depression, discouragement, disappointment, worry, fear, and so on. Never antagonize, never resist what is wrong, and never try to get even. Make the best use of your own talent and the best that is in store for you will positively come your way. When others seem to take advantage of you, do not retaliate by trying to take advantage of them. Use your power in improving yourself, so that you can do better and better work. That is how you are going to win in the race.

Later on, those who tried to take advantage of you will be left in the rear. Remember, those who are dealing unjustly with you or with anybody are misusing their mind. They are therefore losing their power, and will, in the course of time, begin to lose ground; but if you, in the mean time, are turning the full power of your mind to good account, you will not only gain more power, but you will soon begin to gain ground. You will gain and continue to gain in the long run, while others who have been misusing their minds will lose mostly everything in the long run. That is how you are going to win, and win splendidly regardless of ill treatment or opposition.

A great many people imagine that they can promote their own success by trying to prevent the success of other, but it is one of the greatest delusions in the world. If you want to promote your own success as thoroughly as your capacity will permit, take an active interest in the success of everybody, because this will not only keep your mind in the success attitude and cause you to think success all along the line, but it will enlarge your mind so as to give you a greater and better grasp upon the fields of success. If you are trying to prevent the success of others, you are acting in the destructive attitude, which sooner or later will react on others, but if you are taking an active interest in the success of everybody, you are entertaining only constructive attitudes, and these will sooner or later accumulate in your own mind to add volume and power to the forces of success that you are building up in yourself.

In this connection, we may well ask why those succeed who do succeed, why so many succeed only in part, and why so many fail utterly. These are questions that occupy the minds of most people, and hundreds of answers have been given, but there is only one answer that goes to rock bottom. Those people who fail, and who continue to fail all along the line, fail because the power of their minds is either in a habitual negative state, or is always misdirected. If the power of mind is not working positively and constructively for a certain goal, you are not going to succeed. If your mind is not positive, it is negative, and negative minds float with the stream. We must remember that we are in the midst of all kinds of circumstances, some of which are for us and some of which are against us, and we will either have to make our own way or drift, and if we drift we go wherever the stream goes. But most of the streams of human life are found to float in the world of the ordinary and the inferior. Therefore, if you drift, you will drift with the inferior, and your goal will be failure.

When we analyze the minds of people who have failed, we invariably find that they are either negative, non-constructive or aimless. Their forces are scattered, and what is in them is seldom applied constructively. There is an emptiness about their personality that indicates negativity. There is an uncertainty in their facial expression that indicates the absence of definite ambition. There is nothing of a positive, determined nature going on in their mental world.

They have not taken definite action along any line. They are dependent upon fate and circumstances. They are drifting with some stream, and that they should accomplish little if anything is inevitable. This does not mean, however, that their mental world is necessarily unproductive; in fact, those very minds are in many instances immensely rich with possibilities. The trouble is, those possibilities continue to be dormant, and what is in them is not being brought forth and trained for definite action or actual results.

What these people should do is to proceed at once to comply with the three essentials mentioned above, and before many months there will be a turn in the lane. They will soon cease to drift, and will then begin to make their own life, their own circumstances, and their own future. In this connection, it is well to remember that negative people and non-constructive minds never attract that which is helpful in their circumstances. The more you drift, the more people you meet who also drift, while on the other hand, when you begin to make your own life and become positive, you begin to meet more positive people and more constructive circumstances. This explains why "God helps them that help themselves." When you begin to help yourself, which means to make the best of what is in yourself, you begin to attract to yourself more and more of those helpful things that may exist all about you. In other words, constructive forces attract constructive forces; positive forces attract positive forces. A growing mind attracts elements and forces that help to promote growth, and people who are determined to make more and more of themselves are drawn more and more into circumstances through which they will find the opportunity to make more of themselves. And this law works not only in connection with the external world, but also the internal world.

When you begin to make a positive determined use of those powers in yourself that are already in positive action, you draw forth into action powers within you that have been dormant, and as this process continues, you will find that you will accumulate volume, capacity, and power in your mental world until you finally become a mental giant. As you begin to grow and become more capable, you will find that you will meet better and better opportunities, not only opportunities for promoting external success, but opportunities for further building yourself up along the lines of ability, capacity, and talent.

You thus demonstrate the law that "Nothing succeeds like success," and "To him that hath shall be given." And here it is well to remember that it is not necessary to possess external things in the beginning to be counted among them "that hath." It is only necessary in the beginning to possess the interior riches; that is, to take control of what is in you, and proceed to use it positively with a definite goal in view. He who has control of his own mind has already great riches. He has sufficient wealth to be placed among those who have. He is already successful, and if he continues as he has begun, his success will soon appear in the external world. Thus the wealth that existed at first in the internal only will take shape and form in the external. This is a law that is unfailing, and there is not a man or woman on the face of the earth that cannot apply it with the most satisfying results.

The positive and constructive use of the power of mind with a definite goal in view will invariably result in advancement, attainment, and achievement. But if we wish to use that power in its full capacity, the action of the mind must be deep. In addition to the right use of the mind, we must also learn the full use of mind. This implies the use of the whole mind, the deeper mental fields and forces, as well as the usual mental fields and forces.

*Revised and Edited from the works of Larson

Summary of the Philosophy of Wallace Wattles 1910

It is arguable that the definition of wealth is the free and unrestricted use of all of the things that may be necessary for you to advance in the direction of your dreams and potential thus attaining your fullest mental, Spiritual, and physical prosperity.

You have a right to wealth because it is simply a desire for you to have a richer, fuller, and more abundant life. We all should live for the equal advancement and fulfillment of body, mind, and soul, and there is no reason we should limit our capacities in any of the three sectors. Many people see greed, lust, and arrogance in the rich, and wonder if any wealthy people are truly happy. Ironically, poverty can and will frustrate your relationship with Spirit and people, especially with those you love.

Further, poverty creates a negative self-esteem, confidence, and outlook upon life. With poverty of mind and life, you may have nothing to give to those you love and care about, which leads to a very limited life and ability to connect to people and the world. Remember, giving is a form of love and compassion. In sum, abundance and wealth are the same, and if we recognize it and get in tune with it, prosperity will show itself in each of our lives. If you are complacent with your life, then this book is not for you. Stay where you are. Do not advance. Do not exercise your talents to the fullest. Do not leave your gift, mark, or legacy to the world in the form of improvements, opportunity, or education for all.

However, if you want more out of life, and you are tired of failure, we will give you the secrets to success and the keys to prosperity. Why would or should you sit idly by and reject of deny the abundance of the world when it awaits your cooperation and seeking. The world is plentiful with resources, and your creativity is one of the many secrets to your future success. You do not need money to start something, to plan, to begin. You do not need a special talent or to save every penny to be rich. You do not need the perfect business location for your offices. Many people become rich with no talent, no college education, a less than perfect place to work and live, and no start-up capital.

The time is now to change your mind about life and to begin anew. When you are ready and willing to change and open your heart and mind, the gold mine of abundance will be available to you. The whole world of past and present has its eyes on you, waiting for you to achieve your dreams, and all you need to do is make the mental and Spiritual shift in consciousness.

There is plenty of opportunity. Creativity, innovation, and abundance will go to the people who flow and cooperate with life and not reject it. Nature has an inexhaustible source of riches. Accordingly, it is natural to seek more from life, and your advancement is vital for growth. As the old adage states, "We grow or die." On the higher plane and dimension, a person can make forty years worth of advances in three to six years with efficient work. For example, the last one-hundred years has shown more life and technological improvements than the last two-thousand years of civilization.

We will now show you the first secret of life. This key to success can be yours if you simply accept the following statement. Just take it as fact, and the world will begin to move with you.

THOUGHT PRECEEDS FORM

You conceive of your desire, you believe that your goal will happen, and you retrieve the opportunity from the world's storehouse of riches. As a rule, man originates thought. Thought turns into plans or mental images in the mind. Man can communicate his thought and mental images into and throughout the world. This creation begins with our thought focused within and without.

Your mind is the center of your world. The presence of the universal Spirit can be allowed into your mind. Your thoughts mixed with a thankful heart directed toward your inner presence can flow out into the world. You picture and believe that your healthy goal is possible. You understand the essence and reasons that you should have this type of result in your life. You picture your goal with specificity. You think of and picture the opportunity frequently. You believe that you have the type of result that you desire. You feel it and harvest the emotion of having it as much as possible.

These thoughts and a mental practice of visualization will be sent off into the world like a letter of request. If you practice this visualization enough, the desires you have will be met. Truth is your faithful non-doubting interpretation of your thoughts. Do not focus on failure, poverty, disease, or lack. Your truth is health, riches, success, and happiness. Do not doubt your thoughts and dreams. Do not speak against them. Keep these mental petitions as faithful as possible while living harmoniously with people, places, institutions, and the Universe.

It is the desire of the universal Spirit that you should have all that you need. You will begin with a simple desire for some type of improvement in life. A desire coupled with unwavering faith will correctly unfold for you over time. The motives of your desires are important: You want to help yourself and others, and you do not want to hurt other people.

You will achieve these desires much more quickly if your motives are not colored with greed, ego, pride, lust, competition, hate, resentment, and arrogance. Your desires must be propelled by love, gratitude, faith, confidence, mental focus, truth, acceptance, creativity, positive expectation, clear planning, and the giving of more love and value than you take.

TO BEGIN YOUR PROCESS OF PROSPERITY

Brainstorm on your ideas each day. Clarify in you mind exactly what you want and how you will achieve it. Hold the picture of the moment you have completed the achievement with positive certainty. Never speak or think of it as not being possible. Claim it as yours, claim the picture of success as a "FACT" and that it is already yours in mind. Keep your mind tuned in to the universal presence and energy by having a thankful heart and grateful thoughts. If you can not be grateful, then, begin to think of your ability to walk, talk, see, hear, travel, speak, etc. The simplest of freedoms to be grateful for are the most easily overlooked. But, these abilities such as your health are the quickest way to show gratitude and begin a new and powerful positive outlook that connects you to life and your dreams. People will soon not recognize your new outlook and serenity.

Remember, that you must exercise this mental picturing and thankfulness every day for at least a month. However, after a month, you will not believe the difference in your perception of life.

Do not be frightened or ashamed to ask for what you really want. Ask for more than you need. The world is full of people to give and receive. Never be frightened to receive. Receive with humility, thankfulness, and appreciation. Extreme poverty and self-sacrifice are not pleasing to anyone, and extreme altruism is just as dangerous as extreme greed or piety. Thus, give and receive with joy.

We believe that there is a universal Spirit of which unlimited abundance flows. It will give us all that we need and desire when we have a pure heart. A pure heart and mind simply means that you do not allow the weeds of ignorance, bitterness, hate, and irritation to cloud and fill your mind. To facilitate a mind of purity, we make the profound connection to the universal Spirit within us by developing a strong feeling of thankfulness for life, love, health, and our material gifts that we already have or will have.

Let us think about gratitude and thankfulness. Can you have happiness with a bitter heart? Can you have real faith when you are constantly blaming, angry, and ungrateful? If you think you can be happy with a blaming, hateful, and bitter mind, then, good luck. If you want to change to an outlook on life where you feel that all is possible, then keep reading.

Think back and reflect on the times in your life when you got what you wanted and became arrogant or ego centered. After you got what you wanted or got out of a jam, you forgot about and abandoned your connection to your universal Spirit. You may have given up your connection to the Spirit and world because you thought you had won the game of life.

When good things happen to you is the *exact* time that you should exercise and practice having grateful thoughts to continue the flow of riches to us. What you focus on expands. What becomes important to you will come to you and remain with you. If you have doubt and fear, your gratitude will dispel fear and doubt.

Gratitude will keep you connected to the world and affords you a harmonious relationship with all. Gratitude and thankfulness prevent dissatisfaction. Continue to fix your attention on thanks and the best in life. Fix you mind on health, love, success, and good fortune. Your faith will be renewed and strengthened from your exercise of gratitude. It may not happen overnight, but within a month of this simple five-minute-a-day practice, you *will* have results. As an exercise, go a week without complaining. As you may know, complaining attracts destructive people, places, and things into your life. Each time you find yourself complaining, touch each of your shoulders with your finger, and proclaim, "I am abundance."

If you have trouble with certain negative triggers, then eliminate them. If government bothers you, then quit reading the paper for a while. If certain people constantly annoy you, then you should avoid them for a time too. You are working on yourself, and it is OK to take care of your well-being first. The people around you will be happy in the end, if you rebuild and renew your positive Spirit and enthusiasm for life as a priority. This is putting your health first, i.e., your Spiritual health.

Your desires should be very specific. Your mental blueprint must be just as precise. For example, you may write out on a piece of paper a personal contract to yourself:

I, John Doe, Jr., will have a million-dollar business four years from today. I will sell creative *widgets*. I will give the best service and value to my clients. My products and services will have outstanding benefits and will help all of my customers. I will do all of these things, work hard, and be persistent in my service and quality. I will not give up. People will be glad to pay me for my services because they are a benefit to the customer. I will gladly accept payment and do what I need to do to receive the compensation.

Jan. 1, XXXX
John Doe, Jr.
SIGNATURE

Spend each day contemplating your personal contract. Visualize the million-dollar business. Form a mental image of you being paid one million dollars for the business in the form of a check or stock. Mentally imagine yourself on that very moment of completing the transaction with joy. Feel it, harvest the emotion, and believe that an outcome or even better outcome is possible. Moreover, you should know, feel, and see in your mind what you will do when you become rich, how you will live, help others, and serve humanity.

The clearer the picture, the stronger the desire. If your desire is strong, your willingness to focus on the success and claiming it as yours will be made a seamless transaction. You must engage your heartfelt faith to secure a small step to success in each day. Stay engaged and keep moving toward your goals with gratitude and faith. After you have pictured your optimal vision and read your personal agreement to yourself, complete the meditative thought process with the words "and it is so, thank you for the blessing, thank you for expanding the quality of my life, and thank you for protecting me and my family." This will complete your exercise and you then send this petition into the world like a request that must be granted. You should be ready to receive what you want in any form or even a higher form or result.

You need only use your willingness on yourself. You need not think of adversely harming others. You may then always use your self-will to force yourself to think about certain constructive things and doing certain beneficial actions. Every moment in doubt is a waste of time. Direct your attention to prosperity. The best thing you can do for the non-believers is to show them that you can achieve abundance and success. Your creative idea and plan *will* be a success if it is a strong desire that you are willing to go the distance to fulfill your dreams.

Do not tell the same old doubtful people of your plans and ideas. If you tell enough bitter people about your idea, their collective doubt or jealousy may weaken and sabotage your dreams. Surround yourself with experts in the field, people who are encouraging and insightful, people working toward a new outlook on life.

Do not sink into the past by telling others about your difficulties or failures (unless in a secure peer-group where you have at least an unwritten contract of privacy and support). Interest yourself in becoming rich in life! Always try to see the positive side of your present state of affairs. Focus on optimistic conversation or beneficial events that have happened in your life. When you are willing, you must act the part. Do what you need to do. Make lists of things to do and begin doing them one by one. It may take a year to complete, but we must begin somewhere. Do each series of tasks and individual actions efficiently. Do them right the first time, and you need not fix it later. To do efficient and effective work, you need only to do one thing at a time and do not spread yourself too thin. You need not try and mandate an outcome. The creative forces will unfold the correct and highest result for you. You merely need to organize your affairs so that you may receive the success and gladly accept the payoff. Overall, action is what will allow you to receive your abundance. Do only what can be done today, and tomorrow you can begin anew. In sum, put the faith, vision, and purpose behind your every action to accelerate your reaching higher abundance.

FIND OUT WHAT YOU REALLY WANT TO DO AND BE!

You should determine what you like or even what you love to do through this simple process. Write out a list of twenty things of interest to you. Continue adding and subtracting from the list. Over time, you will only have two or three things left because the supreme power will guide you toward your highest given talents. As a note, your purpose could be to study history or science, to read books, to write, to develop written content, to draw or create art and graphics, to travel, or to communicate with people. It should over time become more specific such as: I intend to become the best speaker or writer on the topic of politics or taxes, to complete a masters or doctorate in international business, to build the best Web site for information and links to success literature. It does not matter how you start, just begin the writing process! Just remember, a good talent (something you like to do and you are good at doing) combined with desire to become the best professional in this field will guarantee that you do and be what you love. At the least, you can become a teacher of your trade or profession and give back to the world by accelerating the learning of children or students in your field of love.

Without being boastful, you must convey the impression to others that you are advancing all that come in contact with you. Impress on others that you can add to their lives to promote your goals and ideals. Speak of your life and business as getting better and better all of the time. Act and feel as though you are very successful and that you are already rich in life and all of your needs are met. Incorporate a compassionate humility that you mix with poise, faith, confidence, and self-esteem. You need only speak when necessary, but your strong character and faithful confidence will attract the best people into your life.

If you are in a job and you cannot leave it to immediately follow your dreams, then do what you can in the evenings or weekends to hone your skills, plans, and education toward your goal. Use your present job skillfully to move in the direction that you want. There are thousands of people who have their business pay for their part-time education. Your contacts at work may lead to a better or different job. You must be prepared to discuss your dreams (what you want from life) in spoken words. You must know exactly what you want, and you must clarify and quantify it to others. You must be able to ask for and accept what you want out of life. You will need to interact with others who can help you. This process of abundance, harmonization, and advancement will lead others to want to help you. Be ready for them and be open to forming alliances with them. Thus, your visions, meditations, and requests are traditionally answered by the universal power in the form of another person or entity being available to help and guide you. Be *ready* to tell them what you need, and do not be ashamed to ask for a win-win relationship with the people that come to you.

In conclusion, times are only as good as your mind perceives them. Just when you think you are failing is the exact moment to continue your gratitude, meditation on you goals, and *action*! Just at that moment of doubt is when the highest good for you is ready to unfold. Even if the result is not exactly as you want, something better is very close and coming to you, and you have only been protected from a bad deal or relationship by waiting a little longer.

* Analysis from the Science of Getting Rich – Mentz - Wattles

Contemporary Western Eightfold Path to Abundance

1. Right View

This means to see, interpret, and believe the Highest Truth. It is simple to see things as misery and suffering. It is more noble to see life as a miracle and see beyond what the critical mind can see. The right view affords peace of mind, the ability to take action, and a sense of well-being. We eventually become what we think about all day; thus, our views and how we focus our attention are extremely important. Thinking bigger ideas of abundance, health, love, and so on, is a much greater force than negative ideas. Harmony leads to peace.

2. Right Intention

Intention is also similar to desire or purpose. If we are definite in our intentions and purpose, our dreams can unfold along the lines of our true path. Writing down our intentions is well enough, and has its effect, especially upon ourselves, in clarifying our vision and strengthening our faith; but it is not our oral or written petitions that get us what we want. In order to have abundance we do not need a "minute of prayer and concentration"; we need to "focus without ceasing during all hours." And by focus I mean holding steadily to your vision, with the purpose to cause idea creation into form. We can operate on a plane of mental harmony and good will, and we can flow constructively with life. It is better to not resist everything. We can allow life to unfold in conjunction with our constructive and faithful action. We can make the best of ourselves while in a state of well-being. Our highest truth is harmony, health, and success.

3. Right Speech

Guard and craft your speech carefully. Never speak of yourself, your affairs, or of anything else in a sympathy seeking or discouraging way. Never admit the possibility of failure, or speak in a way that implies disenchantment as a possibility. Never speak of life, career, or the economy as being hard, or of business conditions as being terrible. Times may be hard and business is bad for those who are operating in a Godless scramble within the competitive plane.

You are a constructive creator, your ideas help people, your ideas do not take away from anyone, you can create what you want, and you are above fear. When others are having hard times and poor business, you will find your greatest opportunities. Right speech means the way you talk to others and to yourself. Train yourself to think and speak of life getting better and better with unlimited opportunities. Always speak in terms of advancement; to do otherwise is to deny your faith.

4. Right Action

Every act is, in itself, either effective or inefficient. Every inefficient act is a failure, and if you spend your life in doing inefficient acts, your whole life may become a loss. The more things you do, the worse for you, if all your acts are inefficient ones. On the other hand, if your every action is a success in itself, and if every act of your life is an efficient one, your whole life will be a success. The cause of failure is doing too many things in an inefficient manner without focus, and not doing enough things in an effective manner. You will see that it is a self-evident proposition that if you avoid inefficient acts, and if you do a sufficient number of efficient acts, you will harvest a richer and fuller life. Every action is either strong or weak; and when every one is strong, you are acting in the right way, which allows prosperity for you and your family. Every act can be made strong by holding your vision while you are doing it, and putting the whole power of your love, faith, gratitude, attention, and purpose into it. Further, our minds should facilitate ways and means to capture, receive, and harvest what life has to offer us so that we can use it for our betterment and to help others as well.

Never allow yourself to feel disappointed. You may expect to have a certain thing at a certain time, and not get it at that time; and this will appear as a loss. But if you hold to your faith, you will find that the failure is only apparent. Go on in the mindful way, and if you do not receive that thing, you will receive something so much better that you will see that the seeming loss was really a great success.

5. Right Livelihood

Right livelihood means that one should earn one's living in a Spiritual and joyous way. People should be able to follow their dreams and exercise their God-given talents in the form of livelihood. Therefore, we should be able to work and have fun while being rewarded for what we have given and produced for others. Right livelihood means creating win-win relationships and business dealings where everybody benefits while you use your divine gifts of labor. Your work is for the good of all involved and everyone receives some type of increase and advancement in their lives for interacting with you. Before you become fearful of success, realize that poverty and self-sacrifice are *not* pleasing to God. And, remember that extreme altruism is no better and no nobler than extreme selfishness; both are mistakes. You need not entertain the thought of competition. You are to create, not to compete for what is already created. You do not have to take anything away from any one. You do not have to cheat, obsessively bargain, or to take advantage in negotiations. You do not need to let any man work for you for less than he earns. You do not have to covet the property of others; no man has anything of which you cannot also achieve. You are to become a creator, not a competitor; you are going to get what you want, but in such a way that every other man will have more because of your actions.

6. Right Effort

Right effort can be seen as a prerequisite for the other principles of the path. Without effort, which is in itself an act of will, nothing can be achieved, whereas non-definite effort distracts the mind from its task, and confusion may be the consequence. Thus, you must really desire prosperous effort in your life. The more clear and definite you make your picture of your objectives, the stronger your desire will be; and the stronger your desire, the easier it will be to hold your mental energy fixed upon the picture of what you want. Behind your clear vision must be the purpose to realize it, to bring it out in tangible expression. Right efforts and work mixed with confident expectation or faith will be alive with results.

And behind this purpose must be an invincible and unwavering belief that the thing is already yours, that you already have it in your mind and you need only to take possession of it and receive it with open arms and mind. Live in the new objective, mentally, until it takes form around you physically. No haste is required. However, we know effort is reduced by preparedness. Thus, being ready in your mind, body, and Spirit can enable seamless effort and flow of action. In the mental realm, enter at once into full enjoyment of the things you want. "Whatsoever things ye ask for when ye pray, believe that ye receive them, and ye shall have them," said The Great One.

7. Right Mindfulness

Right mindfulness is the controlled and perfected faculty of cognition. It is the mental ability to see things as they are, with clear consciousness. Usually, the cognitive process begins with an impression induced by perception, or by a thought, but then it does not stay with the mere impression. *A man's way of doing things is the direct result of the way he thinks about things.* To do things in a way you want to do them, you will have to acquire the ability to think the way you want to think; this is the first step toward achieving abundance. *To think what you want to think is to think the truth, regardless of appearances.*

Every man has the natural and inherent power to think what he wants to think, but it requires far more effort to do so than it does to think the thoughts that are suggested by surrounding appearances. To think according to the environment is easy; to think truth regardless of appearances is laborious and requires the expenditure of vast energy, mental power, love, and faith. This is possible for you if you are willing to train yourself and allow yourself to grow along these lines. The more you can harmoniously focus your mind while imagining all of your goal's delightful details, the better. This will bring the Universe in harmony with your highest good, which the Universe must answer for you. Mindfulness also implies that we should be aware that others on this earth are here to help us and may offer assistance. We should be in tune with these opportunities that may come from many places in the form of other people seeking us out.

8. Right Concentration

The eighth principle of the path, concentration, is described as one-pointedness of mind, meaning a state where all mental faculties are unified and directed onto one particular object.

By thought, the thing you most sincerely desire is brought to you; by action you receive it. Hold concentration with faith and purpose. See the vision of yourself in the better environment. Act upon your present environment with all your heart, and with all your strength, and with all your concentration. Hold the vision of yourself with the right outcome or opportunity, with the purpose to get into it, and the faith that you will get into it, and are getting into it; but act in your present opportunity. Use your present situation or business as the means of getting a better one. Your vision of the right purpose or goal, if held with faith and purpose, will cause the Universe to move the right opportunity toward you; and your action, if performed in the light of harmonious intention and concentration, will cause you to move toward the opportunity.

See the things you want as if they were actually around you all the time; see yourself as owning and using them. Make use of them in imagination just as you will use them when they are your tanglble possessions. Dwell upon your mental picture until it is clear and distinct, and then take the mental attitude of ownership toward everything in that picture. Take possession of it, in mind, in the full faith that it is actually yours. Hold to this mental ownership; do not waiver for an instant in the faith that it is real. And remember this about gratitude; be thankful for your life and desires "at all times" as you expect to be when it has taken form. The man who can sincerely thank the Universe for the things he owns only in imagination, has real faith. He will have abundance and peace; he will cause the creation of whatsoever he wants.

Summary of The Eightfold Path

Becoming a warrior at true peace with yourself is the key. Bridging your actions to your Spiritual mind and body is where focus, poise, effectiveness, and success emerge. To advance quickly, man must form a clear and definite mental image of the things he wishes to have, to do, or to become; and he must hold this mental image in his thoughts while being deeply grateful to the Universe that all his highest needs and desires are granted to him. The man who wishes to have an abundant and prosperous life must spend his leisure hours in contemplating his vision, and in earnest thanksgiving that the reality is being given to him. Too much stress cannot be laid on the importance of frequent contemplation of the mental image, coupled with unwavering faith and devout gratitude. This is the process by which the impression is given to the Universe, and the creative forces are set in motion. Your mind will then begin working with you to allow right attention, concentration, and livelihood on a level of love, harmony, faith, and gratitude. Defining your purpose in life or aiming towards specific outcomes while allowing them to unfold in higher and better ways will be where the Spiritual miracles appear. Moreover, allowing your talents, true place, and right career to become part of your life will also be part of your journey. Ultimately, intertwining your concentration, mind, speech, and view to your action will be the missing link of success. Combining the sharpened mind with action is where your daily results begin to add up and build momentum towards growth and expansion.

*Passages compiled from several authors with insights from Prof. Mentz and W. D. Wattles included.

Wealth and Success Techniques for Businesses

Throughout life, there is always a celebrated group of people who succeed and many who fail. What separates the two groups? As an avid reader of success literature and research, there are many psychological, human potential, and even metaphysical strategies advocated to improve our performance or reinvigorate our potential. The irony to life is that we will all need to grow, improve, and change our character and capabilities in any career that we engage in.

To begin this discussion, let us start with the premise that all great businesses begin with an idea. Many businesses are successful by the use of great planning; thus, thoughts can turn into real things. Your thoughts combined with the appropriate desire and plans are the basis of most success. A strong desire is usually what can bring your idea into a reality. So, if you began your business idea with the strong desire to grow and never look back, you probably are successful if you had the persistence to continue through the inevitable cycles of growth. All of us began with some sort of plan of action to grow our business. Some of us had very detailed plans and others did not. Planning is crucial because most people do not define what they will do and are too timid to write down exactly what they want to achieve and how they will realize the goal in any degree of specificity.   Thus, having definite objectives and a specific plan along with a strong desire for success is generally what is needed to accomplish great things. A burning desire is something that you really want to do. You are willing to take action on your burning desire and develop an action plan. You should have faith that you can make your plan happen. You are willing to sever the past and move forward with your objectives and desires. You are willing to focus your attention and positive emotions almost exclusively on this career project, and never give up. Having your stated objectives while engaging positive thoughts, enthusiasm, and persistence that is built on honesty and integrity will propel your business growth.

In this next section, there are clear bullet points that describe an easy exercise to define your plan. This involves putting pen to paper. On paper, you will write out clearly what you want to achieve.

George Mentz, JD, MBA

Be Specific:

How to Create a Personal Agreement with Yourself by Firmly Establishing What You Want.   Write Your Plan in Specific Terms by Determining the Following:

- Write what you desire to accomplish (the amount of clients or dollars under management or annual salary).
- Write what service, time commitment, and value that you will give to earn and deserve the outcome.
- Write how you will conduct and arrange your life and business to allow the receipt of prosperity and compensation.
- Write the date your goal will be achieved.
- Sign and date the written plan or contract with yourself
- Read the plan daily upon beginning your work day and before retiring for the evening.
- Frequently feel that you have achieved success in heart and mind, and harvest that emotion of attainment.
- Imagine what you will do with your success after you acquire success.

Enthusiasm and faith can be induced through several practices or exercises: Enthusiasm and a proactive attitude are some of the major forces that when coupled with your desire can propel a plan.

As for the metaphysical aspect of success: Many professionals use these technique for a few minutes a day to reaffirm their personal faith and success mentality so that they will indeed accomplish what they desire.

- Find a quiet spot to relax.
- Read statements of desire (think about your personal objectives in you minds eye).
- Practice forming mental images of your personal success in your spare time.
- Project the image of your success on the subconscious mind using a heart felt emotion. See that you have success already in your imagination: For example, imagine yourself with a salary five times what it is today and feel the emotions of achieving that goal at year-end. We stress that you do this daily.
- Use affirmations: reading aloud the professional and successful attributes that you desire such as: "I am a great professional and deserve to have great clients. (Or you should read your personal agreement statement frequently.)
- Use gratitude and thankfulness of heart. As many success writers state, "Complaining and being negative is a waste of your time and energy." Moreover, when being thankful for your job, career, clients, health and so forth, you will create an energy of attraction that will bring you more positive outcomes, happiness, and success. Further, new clients and your existing clients will be more attracted to your successful and positive outlook. Believe me, clients can sense this. Therefore, you should contemplate the good in your life while relaxing and having a sense of well-being.
- Combine the above with action, action and more action. See below.

A Successful Action Plan

- Your actions must be persistent. This means that you should be proactive in building new business as well as keeping satisfied customers.
- Avoid lack of decision and procrastination and stick with your decision and plan. An example of this would be to let go of a bad client if managing this relationship is consistently abusing your time and energy without just rewards and payment for your time.
- Write down each day what you will do to move forward with your business plans. Be efficient and effective. Do all you can do each day without haste. Do not worry about yesterday or tomorrow. Today, you should accomplish all you can. Over time, this adds up, and you will receive positive results in your business.
- Strong thoughts of gratitude and enthusiasm will bring about change for the better in you and your environment. This simply means to focus what you desire and on being the best and thinking about the best for you, your family, and your business.
- Organize your affairs so that you can receive the rewards of a better business. Thus, allow for new and better clients. Believe that you deserve them. Do not be afraid to charge them value for value. This may mean acquiring greater business tools, administrative assistance, infrastructure use, and ways to capture income. This may also entail offering a broader line of products or services. In any event, be prepared to provide solutions and do the homework before asking for the free lunch.
- Surround yourself with encouraging professional mentors or advisors.
- Know in your heart that an outcome similar to what you expect or something even better will come to you at the right time.

Professional Growth and Mentor Groups:

- Develop a group of friends who can give you professional insight and feedback and will support your goals and share their own personal experiences and success tactics.
- You should be willing to help all members in this group of professional friends with your knowledge, skill, and support.
- Meet often for planning and to obtain and give feedback to your group.

You must always speak and act to maintain harmony with this group with positive and encouraging conversation. Thus, never belittle or constantly contradict your group members. Offer solutions, not criticism.

Belief in Yourself, Your Products, and Service:

Believe that your products and services are as good or better than any products available. Know the details of your products and services. Be able to articulate the benefits of your service. Chances are that what you sell is just as good as what the competition offers. Your products and services create opportunity for clients. Do not be afraid to sign up the new business client, because someone else will do this if you do not. Moreover, remember that some small clients take just as much time to manage as do very large clients. Therefore, time management is essential. As they say, "Over time, it is better to have twenty great accounts than one-hundred-fifty non-productive customers."

Being Successful

In my career, I have helped many people. I feel great joy in contributing to anyone's financial freedom. Moreover, I realize that many of you are great successes already and commend all of you. With success, there is usually hard work and many people who depend on you. As a reminder, there will be times when you just need to rest, relax, or take a vacation. There will be seasons where you may need to rejuvenate your enthusiasm for your business. With all of that being said, your physical and mental well-being is the most important thing to maintain so that you may continue all of your good works. Therefore, try to keep a balance with body, mind, and soul and incorporate good exercise, diet, leisure, and rest with your professional life.

21St Century – Laws of Abundance Teachings

#1 Cause and Effect "Your actions and the reactions of the World"

You must be aware of your choices of mind and action.

With each action, you should be able to ask the following question: "What are the potential consequences of this Choice?" To begin with, constructive actions will create and build opportunity and positive outcomes. View each choice with the end result in mind. Your choices allow you to mentally visualize or feel the outcome. Therefore, you can judge the circumstance or end result in your mind's eye and in your heart. With each choice there are questions. Will it bring me peace of mind? Right action is the right response or choice for any given situation or moment. Some of us can ask our body, heart, or Spiritual center if the choice is right. Does the choice allow us to feel comfortable sensations in our Spirit? The area of the center body gives tiny emotions or feelings that will help us make decisions if we ask in mind and heart so that we can feel our inner response. With our individual journey we can have times of joy and hardship resulting from any decision. We must be able to ask ourselves what we have learned from our journey or choices. Be aware of your choices with mindfulness. Then, try and make decisions, take action, and move ahead with your journey.

#2 Allow Your True Place to Appear

We must live according to providence. There are things that we are meant to do. We must dig deep into our souls to determine what our true purpose on earth is. Our being wants us to live and express our true talents and inner desires. You may have a dream to build hospitals, write poetry or create music. You may even have a calling to minister to the sick or poor. Whatever it is, be sure and express this before you leave this world. Many people find this true place in their labor. They call this a "labor of love
 or "right livelihood". This type of joyous work is easy and enjoyable regardless of how stressful it may be for others. This is because your purpose energizes your work and you are *having fun*.

#3 Flow of Life and Love Energy: Giving and Receiving

Circulate your energy and Spiritual flow by giving. By giving, we receive. By doing more than the cosmos expects us to do, we are rewarded by the unbounded goodness of Karma.

Give something to all persons such as the following: kind thoughts, compliments, affection, gifts of no real monetary value, compassion, radiations of your love, or bless them mentally. Giving should be unconditional without wild expectations of return of any favors or the like. Your harmonious and loving action towards others will be received and complimented in many ways. Mostly, your reward will be peace and joy, but most often, the fruits of flow come from other people who are not even related to the recipient of the initial gifts. After giving, you must be capable of receiving. Receive life's gifts and remain truly open to receive compliments, things, help, love, or even money.

#4 Prayer, Contemplation, Meditation, Self-Evaluation

What do we want from life? We want more happiness and an ability to fulfill desires. Most of us desire abundance and a flow of goodness into our lives. In the larger scheme of life, we want and desire health and a rich life in the physical, Spiritual, and mental realms. We want peace of mind and to nurture our Spirituality. Some believe that true success is the unfolding of our Spiritual life where oneness is attained with all.

The source is the Spirit and the process is the mind. We are Spiritual mind. With the mind, we have unlimited possibilities of creative thinking. Fear and doubt is also creative but limits possibilities because it can cause paralysis in your growth. Ego and control is also a block to Spiritual growth and connection with higher powers.

Real power is pure, without fear, and fueled by love. Meditation, silence, and simply being are the first and primary ways to engage and receive pure power. Non-judgment creates peace in mind. Spiritual masters often suggest that you try and not judge others just for the day in thought, word, and deed.

Further, many authors recommend meditation for thirty minutes a day, twice a day. While doing so, listen to your inner and creative thoughts and intuition that come from silence. Many teachers suggest communing with nature and becoming aware of nature. Thus, open your eyes to creation. From an internal standpoint great teachers often reveal that all external relationships are a mirror of relationship with your inner self. Therefore, it is critical to obtain inner peace so that you are at peace with others. Mastering this will allow you to respond to others with awareness and compassion. With self-realization comes wealth. What is wealth? The essence of wealth is being blessed with life energy or the Holy Spirit, and you will know it when this occurs.

George Mentz, JD, MBA

A Summary of the Science of Getting Rich Metaphysics

There is a spiritual energy and force in every thought, from which all things are made, and which, in its original state, permeates, penetrates, and fills the interspaces of the Universe. A thought in this substance produces the thing that is imaged by the thought. Persons can form things in his their thought, and by impressing their thoughts upon formless substance (interspaces of the Universe) can cause the thing he they think about to be created. In order to do this, people must pass from the competitive to the creative mind. Otherwise they cannot be in harmony with formless intelligence, which is always creative and never competitive in Spirit.

People may come into full harmony with the formless substance by entertaining a lively and sincere gratitude for the blessings it bestows upon them. Gratitude unifies the mind of man with the intelligence of substance, so that man's thoughts are received by the formless. People can remain upon the creative plane only by uniting themselves with the formless intelligence through a deep and continuous feeling of gratitude.

People must form a clear and definite mental image of the things they wish to have, to do, or to become, and they must hold this mental image in his their thoughts while being deeply grateful to the supreme that all his their desires are granted. People who wish to get rich must spend their leisure hours in contemplating their vision, and in earnest thanksgiving that the reality is being given to them.

Too much stress cannot be laid on the importance of frequent contemplation of the mental image, coupled with unwavering faith and devout gratitude. This is the process by which the impression is given to the formless and the creative forces set in motion.

The creative energy works through the established channels of natural growth, and of the industrial and social order. All that is included in his mental image will surely be brought to people who follow the instructions given above, and whose faith does not waver. What they want will come to them through the ways of established trade and commerce.

In order to receive their own when it is ready to come to them, people must be in action in a way that causes them to more than fill their present place. They must keep in mind the purpose to get rich through realization of their mental image. And they must do, every day, all which can be done that day, taking care to do each act in a successful manner. They must give to every person a use value in excess of the cash value they receive, so that each transaction makes for more life, and they must hold the advancing thought so that the impression of increase will be communicated to all with whom they comes into contact.

The men and women who practice the foregoing instructions will certainly get rich, and the riches they receive will be in exact proportion to the definiteness of their vision, the fixity of their purpose, the steadiness of their faith, and the depth of their gratitude. *Wallace D. Wattles (1910) – Enhanced by Prof. Mentz*

Exercises to Augment Awareness and Mental Abilities

First, get in a quiet place where there are no distractions and think of the alphabet. Think of a letter. Select the letter "J" for instance. Think of a person in your family or in your childhood with a "J" in their name who you were very fond of or even loved. Ponder that loving emotion. Think of the happy times you had with this person. Bless that person in your mind. Consider the ability to transfer this feeling to another person in your current life.

Second, think of a color, for example, blue. Think of something blue that you owned that gave you happiness in the past. Harvest that emotion. Feel it. Try and re-live the joy of having the thing.

Third, consider one of the five senses (tasting, touching, smelling, hearing, seeing). Select one, such as smell. Remember your favorite aroma. Think back about the flavor or pleasant smell. Ponder the joys of enjoying that aroma again, for example, a great cup of espresso in Venice, Italy. Experience the moments in the past that you enjoyed in conjunction with the feeling and senses. Allow gratitude to fill the mind, Spirit, and body.

Fourth, consider the following several methods to achieve the harmonious relationship with your world to be in tune with spiritual abundance:

- ➢ Start blessing and praising what is yours.
- ➢ Harvest a thankful heart and mind for all of your good fortune such as the ability to do simple things such as think, taste, smell, hear, see, and do, and more.
- ➢ Get into nature and wilderness to be still and feel the presence.
- ➢ Take a moment to sit or kneel and make a prayer of thanksgiving.
- ➢ Write out a list of things that you are thankful for and keep them in your wallet to read whenever you need to refocus on how you are truly blessed and protected by the Universe.
- ➢ Quit complaining and begin praising or complimenting others.
- ➢ Complement or praise somebody or a family member.
- ➢ Think of a person who was truly kind to you.
- ➢ Try and remember a person who you think really loves you.
- ➢ Think of all those who love or care for you now.
- ➢ Do something for another person to help him or her, or simply write the person a letter or give him or her a flower.
- ➢ Spend time with a spouse, loved one, or child and focus only on wonderful, beautiful, encouraging thoughts about this person.

Fifth, See Yourself in Your Mind's Eye

 ➢ See yourself doing what you want to do. Imagine a labor of love.
 ➢ See yourself living where you want to live.
 ➢ See yourself fulfilled in your relationships
 ➢ Act, feel, and think as if you are whom you want to be. This will assist in the growth and enhancement of your total character in reaching Spiritual abundance.

Imagine yourself in the occupation of your dreams. What would it be like? How would you feel? Harvest the emotion of having all you desire.

The mind's eye is the picture screen of creation. The more clearly and powerfully you project your images in and onto your consciousness and then to your subconscious, the more easy it will be for your ideals and goals to manifest. As a secret teaching, I would imagine exactly what you want with specificity. Imagine successfully earning the best outcome. Then, I would project that image and feeling into the world, like sending out a letter. Imagine the exact completed successful outcome. You are finished and you can do this exercise later or each day until you have achieved your desire.

A SPIRITUAL EXERCISE FOR HEALTH.

A Spiritual exercise is a simple metaphysical methodology, not just in repeating words, but in the thinking of certain thoughts. Allowing these thoughts to permeate your being and sense and feel the thoughts will eventually allow them to become part of you. The words that we repeatedly say and hear become convictions. As Goethe says, the thoughts that we repeatedly think become habitual, and make us what we are. Moreover, Goethe implied that thoughts intertwined with character will enhance our action and boldness. The purpose in taking a mental exercise is that you may think certain thoughts repeatedly until you form a habit of thinking them, then they will be your thoughts all the time. Taken in the right way and with an understanding of their purpose, mental and Spiritual exercises are of great value. The thoughts embodied in the following exercise are the ones you want to think. You should take the exercise once or twice daily, but you should muse over the thoughts continuously. That is, do not think them twice a day for a stated time and then forget them until it is time to take the exercise again. The exercise is to impress you with the formulation for continuous thought. Take a time when you can have from twenty minutes to half an hour secure from interruption and proceed first to make yourself physically comfortable. Rest at ease in a recliner, chair, bed, or on a couch; it is best to lie flat on your back.

If you have no other time, take the exercise on going to bed at night and before rising in the morning. First let your attention travel over your body from the crown of your head to the soles of your feet, relaxing every muscle as you go. Relax completely. And next, get physical and other ills off your mind. Let attention pass down the spinal cord and out over the nerves to the extremities, and as you do so think to yourself: My nerves are in perfect order all over my body. They obey my will, and I have great nerve force.

Next bring your attention to the lungs and think: I am breathing deeply and quietly, and the air goes into every cell of my lungs, which are in perfect condition. My blood is purified and made clean. Next, to the heart: My heart is beating strongly and steadily, and my circulation is perfect, even to the extremities. Next, to the digestive system: My stomach and bowels perform their work perfectly. My food is digested and assimilated and my body rebuilt and nourished. My liver, kidneys, and bladder each perform their several functions without pain or strain; I am perfectly well. My body is resting, my mind is quiet, and my soul is at peace. I have no anxiety about financial or other matters. God, who is within me, is also in all things I want, impelling the highest good toward me; all that I want is already given to me. I have no anxiety about my health, for I am perfectly well. I have no worry or fear whatever. I rise above all temptation of moral evil. I cast out all greed, selfishness, and narrow personal ambition; I do not hold envy, malice, or enmity toward any living soul. I will follow no course of action that is not in accord with my highest ideals. I am right and I will do right.

KEEPING THE HIGHEST VIEWPOINT WITHIN AND WITHOUT

All is right with the world. It is perfect and advancing to completion. I will contemplate the facts of social, political, and industrial life only from this high viewpoint. Behold, life and the world is all very good. I will see all human beings, all my acquaintances, friends, neighbors, and the members of my own household in the same way. They are all good. Nothing is wrong with the Universe or my world; nothing can be wrong but my own personal attitude, and henceforth I keep that right. My whole trust is in the Supreme Master.

CONSECRATION OF THE EXERCISE.

I will obey my Inner Spirit and be true to what within me is highest. I will search within for the pure idea of right and good in all things, and when I find it I will express it in my outward life. I will abandon everything I have outgrown for the best I can think. I will have the highest thoughts concerning all my relationships, and my manner, character, and action shall express these thoughts inwardly and outwardly. I will surrender my body to be ruled by my mind; I yield my mind to the dominion of my higher source, and I give my soul to the guidance of my higher power. * *Wallace Wattles (1910) Enhanced by Prof. Mentz*

Metaphysical Issues & Insights

Harmonious Relationships:

Connected with all there is that is good, harvesting and having a harmonious relationship with the world through various philosophical exercises, using gratitude for any of your gifts on a daily basis can grow your expectation of good and faith. It is much easier to be connected when you have set aside or removed destructive thinking such as resentments, jealously or the seven deadly sins.

Desires

Desires are good and excellent. Desires can focus you on enriching your life and following your true direction. Cultivating desires into reality is vital for change, innovation, and improvement. You would not have a desire unless it was possible, but select desires where you have a solid sphere of possibility. An earnest and heartfelt desire is what allows us to seize upon opportunities and develop plans.

Plans

A plan or objective is fundamental in the clarification and specificity of your desire. A large majority of people are afraid to specify what they intend to do. Transcending this fear and taking bold action upon your plans and strategies allows for the growth and manifestation of your idea into a reality

Vision

A vision is important in that you clarify the path to your short-term and long-term enrichment of yourself, your goals, teamwork, or relationships.

Mission

A mission is important in that you can quantify and clarify a path to an outcome or ending strategy.

Having, Emotion, and Feelings

Mentally understanding the outcome or result as if you have it already is very important. It also allows you to qualify the consequences. It further provides you with feelings surrounding the outcome. Harvesting positive feelings surrounding the outcome is very important to energize a desire, mission, visualization, and result.

Visualization, Pictures, Imagination, Sending It Out

Mental visualization of your objectives holds great importance in the clarity of what you intend to do along the way and what you desire as an end result. Seeing what you intend to do and what you desire and plan as if it is real is a complex mental exercise, but vital to the codification and building of the objective so as to assist the manifestation of the result. Seeing *exactly* what you desire and intend causes you to specify your wants and desires. The stronger and longer you can hold your ideal in your mind's eye, the better.

Attention Focus

Pointing your mental faculties toward the individual actions required to achieve a task, project, or goal is what causes effectiveness, as long as your acts are efficient. Continuous and persistent thinking and action toward your work, goal, project, or desired outcome can funnel or intensify the energy in a specific direction.

Efficiently and Effectively

Completion and closure of acts and tasks one-by-one in a successful manner is what creates momentum toward an objective with no need to go backward.

Presence, Awareness, Doing

Thinking and planning are most crucial. However, boldness and action are what may cause events to happen and people to be attracted to you. Therefore, contemplation mixed with action is the optimal, blended solution.

Cause/Effect: "Like Attracts Like"

Every action has a reaction. Types of actions and thoughts attract similar actions and thoughts. Kindness tends to bring kindness. Respect tends to bring respect. Additionally, constructive thinking tends to bring constructive opportunities and events to the individual.

Increase

All mankind tends to be attracted to those who can bring them more life or enrichment. If an individual projects life and opportunity, then he or she will attract similar minds.

Insight and Restraint

Insight and restraint contain the ability to think something over, discuss it with others, or seek out counsel from others who understand or know the subject well without acting hastily. Thus, the opinion of experts and consequences are a valid consideration in thinking and acting.

Love, Forgiveness, Harmony, Dissipating Discouragement

Cultivating love and forgiveness can dispel otherwise destructive thoughts. Great minds can look back on things they love or loved, and re-harness that emotion.

Minding Your Own Business

There is something very real in taking care of yourself and your affairs. As such, your enhanced mind, body, soul, and financial affairs allow you to help those whom you love and serve humanity in better ways. The best way to be of service to humanity and your loved ones is to make the best of yourself.

Gratitude, Enthusiasm, Faith

A sincere heartfelt gratitude for life and its gifts will allow the flow of good to you. Systematic recognition of people or things to be thankful for along with gratitude may facilitate an expectation of good and growth of inherent faith. Integrating this confident expectation with your aspirations creates great power.

Guarded Speech, Response/Ability

Speaking of only positive things can attract opportunity and friends. Keeping your desires and goals close to you will keep them from becoming dissipated energy. Sharing your desires and goals with those who support, encourage, and assist you can be a positive exercise and help harvest constructive feedback.

Change/Insanity

Not evolving while continuing to do things that are failures or destructive actions tends to prevent any growth.

Creating Versus Competing

It seems that many people feel that competition causes a limited supply. However, from a supply or abundance standpoint, individuals can create without competing, to serve humanity. As an example, an individual who creates a new cure to solve a common health problem is not competing against the world, but helping it.

Right Livelihood and Labor of Love

Having a labor of love can cause effectiveness and efficiency through energetic work. Doing something that you believe in or selling a product that you have faith in, can make your job much easier or even fun. Having fun with work is a divine right.

Blessing, Praise, Protection, and Expansion

Persons who engage in a metaphysical approach seem to enjoy a greater state of well-being and success when they bless their relationship with the Universe, bless their loved ones, bless their home, and give thanks for their health on a daily basis.

Gratitude, Religion and Great Thinkers

If the only prayer you say in your life is "Thank you," that would suffice. --**Meister Eckhart**

Take full account of the excellencies which you possess, and in gratitude remember how you would hanker after them, if you had them not. --**Marcus Aurelius**

The Holy Koran, which is divided into sections called *suras*, repeatedly asserts the necessity for gratitude and thankfulness to God. For example, in Sura fourteen it is written: "If you are grateful, I will give you more "(14:7). A traditional Islamic saying states, "The first who will be summoned to paradise are those who have praised God in every circumstance." The prophet Muhammad also stated, "Gratitude for the abundance you have received is the best insurance that the abundance will continue." True gratitude, it is taught, draws more abundant graces upon the believer.

Judaism

In the Jewish faith, gratitude is a critical component of worship. In the Hebrew Scriptures, the Psalms are saturated with thanksgiving to God: "O Lord my God, I will give thanks to you forever" (30:12), and "I will give thanks to the Lord with my whole heart "(9:1).

Christianity

In the Christian faith, Philippians IV sums up the Christian attitude toward gratitude. See Below:

Philippians IV

4 Rejoice in the Lord always. Again I will say, rejoice! 5 Let your gentleness be known to all men. The Lord [is] at hand. 6 Be anxious for nothing, but in everything by prayer and supplication, with thanksgiving, let your requests be made known to God; 7 and the peace of God, which surpasses all understanding, will guard your hearts and minds through Christ Jesus. 8 Finally, brethren, whatever things are true, whatever things [are] noble, whatever things [are] just, whatever things [are] pure, whatever things [are] lovely, whatever things [are] of good report, if [there is] any virtue and if [there is] anything praiseworthy -- meditate on these things. 9 The things which you learned and received and heard and saw in me, these do, and the God of peace will be with you. 10 But I rejoiced in the Lord greatly that now at last your care for me has flourished again; though you surely did care, but you lacked opportunity. 11 Not that I speak in regard to need, for I have learned in whatever state I am, to be content: 12 I know how to be abased, and I know how to abound. Everywhere and in all things I have learned both to be full and to be hungry, both to abound and to suffer need. 13 I can do all things through Christ who strengthens me.

Read the above statements and passages from the Old Scriptures and other quotes and think about: gentleness, thanksgiving, constructive petitions, request for blessings, a sincere feeling of gratitude, meditating on noble and optimistic thoughts, rejoicing in life, and even blessing yourself and your future.

Unfolding Detachment Protected for Higher Good

When we become too attached or dependent on an external person, place, thing, or result, we can become disappointed with other people and things. It is good to expect the best, but it is also smart to allow for something better to unfold. Thus, trying to control a specific outcome without any flexibility can inhibit the Universe from its creativity.

Receiving, Valuing, Deserving

Many people from around the world feel unworthy of abundance. Many people do not value themselves, their service, their talents, and work. It is very important to learn to feel worthy, unique, and deserving of good. Moreover, you should become mentally open to receiving all good in life. Further, people should be careful to create ways to receive the good into their lives from the Universe and from others. Example: Accepting a compliment from another person.

Other People and When They Are Sent to Help You

When you engage a mentality of abundance and harmonious Spiritual thinking, your mind will expand and increase while radiating love, abundance, and health. Thus, your powers of attraction will increase. The Universe will send people to help you. It will be your job to select and allow them to assist you in a win-win relationship to expand your abundance where all can achieve a richer and fuller life through these joint ventures.

Resistance and Flow

Types of resistance that inhibit your abundance, health, and connection with Spirit are: resentment, jealousy, anger, judgment, criticism, hatred, greed, pride, and mental laziness. Other subtle resistance is to institutions, conformity, and adapting. It is better to adapt than to perish, while maintaining your unique qualities

Willingness

Willingness is the key to advancement. Be willing to take action, take a chance, or risk failure or embarrassment. Without willingness, you may never engage mental, Spiritual, or physical action that leads to good. Willingness is a vital ingredient toward successful visualization, belief, action, planning, and success. Am I willing to believe, to try, to risk, to engage? Can it be done? And why not?

Hoarding and Change

Holding onto old ideas, old things, and old ways can keep you from growth, Spiritual flow, and expansion. Taking an inventory of mental ideas and material things must be done. Eliminating the ideas, things, people, and actions that create inconvenience, frustration, clutter, and resentment will allow freedom and harmony in your life.

Recognition of Cause

It can be a fundamental mistake if you give yourself too much credit for anything good that you receive from life. Additionally, it can be a disastrous mistake to continue to blame God and the Universe for anything bad that you receive from life.

Sanity, Root Out Cause, Unlimited Potential

Root out the cause of your failures, your inconveniences, your frustration, and your mental or Spiritual disabilities. If you have a problem, there may be a cause. If you injured yourself engaging in a specific activity, you may avoid this activity in the future or better prepare for it next time. Otherwise, you may pay for this repeated action in the form of more pain and suffering. If you have a relationship that always seems to leave you in pain, then you may need to avoid this person if you are spiritually whole and the other person is not.

Giving Without Expectation, Tithing

Taking time to give money, service, or goods to divine recipients will create an untold flow in your life. Life requires circulation of your ideas, your things, and your service to humanity. With this giving, it is virtually guaranteed that your life will be blessed and protected through your giving of yourself. You are not doing this to take advantage of the law. You do this to expand your Spiritual existence, keep the flow, and give back. Expecting something in return is not needed because the Universe will provide opportunity for you by your embracing this process.

Wasting Energy and Thought

If you become frustrated every time you watch the news or read the newspaper, then why would you continue to read a specific article or watch that particular channel? It is vitally important for you to engage relaxing or strengthening activities rather than getting the same shot of bad medicine each day.

Good Deeds and Action / Balance Karma

You may feel you have wronged many people. You may even feel guilty for past deeds or encounters. However, if you feel remorse and intend to act as a better person for now on, then you have made progress. In any event, your day-to-day action and character of goodness and kindness will build your positive energy where the world has decided to protect you and serve you.

Meek Defined: Open Mind, Faith in Universe, Will of God, Spirit Before Ego

Meek is not weak. It is strong, confident, cooperative, and advantageous. Developing an honest appraisal of yourself can be healthy. You can always improve yourself, your credentials, your relationships and your business. Putting your ego first can be dangerous. When somebody has hurt your feelings, said you are wrong, said "no" to you, or otherwise attacked you, it is best to analyze (when possible) and discuss the issue with another supportive person before retaliating with e-mail, phone, letter, or in person.

Peace and Serenity Are Needed for Concentration

Peace allows growth. Clarity and concentration are primary keys to serenity. Being able to operate on a plane with singleness of mind can allow you to achieve great things. A person who cannot focus and achieve one thing at a time may never cross "the finish line" with any dream, goal, or aspiration. Overall, if you allow resentment, frustration, hate of another, or fear to dominate your thoughts, then your effectiveness will be diminished. Hard work is required to keep you focused and concentrating on bettering yourself. Overall, your freedom, vitality and wholeness depend on your effectiveness.

Visualizing Completed Transaction With Joy

We have mentioned visualization. Do not forget that you should visualize things and plans as you would have them. You should believe that they are yours in mind. Paint your ideal outcome on the mental screen in your mind's eye. Believe that it is completed. Fuse your image with love and gratitude. Celebrate its reception in your mind. Believe that you have the proper channels to receive what is coming to you. Send your vision and petition into the Universe and repeat the exercise for fantastic results.

Treasure Map and Wheel of Fortune

If you cannot paint the mental picture as clearly as you would want, then try to use the material world to enhance your mind. Cut out pictures of the ideal things you want. Put them into a collage or on poster board. Rip out images of the home you desire, people having fun, distant places that you want to visit, or the lifestyle and types of relationships that you desire. This action can help you amalgamate the images to imprint them on your subconscious mind. View them daily and place them in a prominent place. Overall, imagine having these things in your quite time. Sense the joy of receiving all of it fully.

Attraction by Thoughts

As for attraction, this can be of mind, action, and omission. You can think of something all day and possibly attract this. Further, you may act a certain way and either become it or attract it in your life. Moreover, your omissions of conduct may prevent you from steering into the direction of your life dreams.

When you consider your close family relationships, you may want to reevaluate how you respond to family members' mistakes, ideas, and thoughts. If you respond in a dubious fashion, your family members may not want to tell you about themselves. If your conversations are always woeful and negative, then your family members may consider you a toxic person. As such, if you are predisposed to being negative and a contrarian, you would probably attract others who seek to discuss the same theme with you or even try to better you in the experience of misery and misfortune. Also, your omissions are important also. If you refuse to help anyone, you may not be helped when you need it. If you omit tolerance and love to others, you may not receive it either. Thus, there is a delicate balance of give and take in the world. It is better to give now and then you shall be given to and provided for as time goes on.

With all of this in mind, it is far more practical to look at the possibilities of success, good ideas, magic, miracles, and more in others. See the God and genius in all of those you love and around you, and maybe it will be revealed and vitalized to and within you.

4 Keys to Peace and Success

#1 The Law of Spiritual Resistance

Detachment and Non-resistance means to not resist moving ahead in harmony with the currents of life while maintaining and growing a sense of peace. Not allowing simple external things to hold you back. How do you achieve flow? Great teachers discuss many methods of relaxation or meditation. Men commune with nature at times to reflect on life, atone, or tune into the universal Spirit. Many Spiritual masters sincerely believe that giving attention to the source of all is vitally important.

Further, they imply that it is highly important to develop a harmonious relationship with the Universal Spirit or Force. This can be done, of course, through the cultivation of gratitude, prayer, and meditation. Moreover, through living a life of love, tolerance, and peace, our actions will bring us closer to the source of all.

Overall, people who actively engage a Spiritual life can become very efficient and effective because they are focused and have a state of well-being. Thus, the very experienced soul can do much less work to achieve the same degree of success as the average soul. When a person is in harmony and non-resistance with the world and motivated by love and joy, life will flow to him or her with powerful rewards. Overall, the body generates and expends energy. Selfishness and the desire to control others is a great waste of precious energy. Seeking validation and approval from everyone is also a big waste of energy. Becoming who you really are is a lifelong journey. In sum, doing esteemed actions will create esteem in your life. Unfolding to your highest level will be your reward.

Some Elements of The Law Cause and Effect:

➢ Acceptance of people, places, and things. Find the good in all. Develop gratitude for what is good in all things.
➢ Take responsibility for things as they are, and quit blaming external forces.
➢ Cultivate constructive thoughts and mental energy. Focus your thoughts on what you do want and *not* on what you do not want.
➢ Truly feel gratitude and allow emotions of thankfulness and constructive expectation to emerge from within.
➢ Feel gratitude for what you desire as if you had it already.
➢ See in your mind's eye what you want, send it into the Universe like a letter of thanks.
➢ Relinquish the need to argue with others regarding your point of view. This saves and builds energy.
➢ Remain open minded and willing for life to unfold in abundance.
➢ Keep specific goals, but release your desire to control exact outcomes, because the Universe may provide a better result than you could have possibly hoped for.

#2 The Manifestation of Your Dreams.

Your body is part of the Universe and the Universe is an extension of your body. Both influence each other. You are connected to all through energy. Therefore, your mind and Spirit are directly linked to the world. Your consciousness allows you to effect and cooperate with the Universe. Focus your attention on what you really want from life and believe that it is possible. The quality of your focus and your intent has great power. Attention plus real burning desire allows you to forge ahead, organize plans, and complete major tasks. You must do all of this with a sense of love, thankfulness, and a desire to benefit mankind.

Attention, intent, and desires should have fixity of purpose. This means to hold attention on a positive outcome. Avoid directing your attention toward your obstacles and hardships. These difficulties can be changed to opportunities if you are paying attention.

Some Steps to Manifesting Your Desire:

- ➢ Go into silence.
- ➢ Focus your attention upon your dreams and objectives.
- ➢ Release your carefully chosen desires.
- ➢ Do not be influenced by others' opinions, and keep your specific desires to yourself.
- ➢ Cultivate gratitude toward the world and allow the universe to help you.
- ➢ Relinquish attachment or anxiety toward the exact outcome.
- ➢ Allow a higher or better outcome to come into your life.
- ➢ Make a list of your desires and read them each day and night.
- ➢ Pay attention to people, places, and things that are sent to assist you in your journey.

#3 The Laws of Release and Cooperation

Relinquish attachment and surrender your desires to the greater all. But, you should still maintain your desire, attention, and focus. Just continue to *send* the desire into the greater world with great faith, much like sending a mental telegram to the great force. Releasing allows you to continue to create and improve on your original desire as you go along.

There is a big materialistic flaw in this Philosophy – "When I get the next thing, I will be happy." This type of statement can be destructive because it can become a cycle of frustration, and we may never be satisfied. Thus, work hard and allow life to unfold while not being be too controlling, i.e., be flexible. In sum, allow all of the best possibilities or alternatives, and try not to force things to happen, staying alert to the options and possibilities.

When you are prepared and meet the options that life gives you, this is excellent fortune.

#4 Success in the Now

There is not other time but now. Your truth is what is here but sometimes beyond what you may see. We must stay aware to opportunity and possibility today. Yesterday and tomorrow cannot be acted upon today. Seek joy and happiness now. Allow your mind to engage bliss and contentment. In this day, you can do what is necessary toward your dreams and goals. However, be your best and do what you do well. As time moves forward, your harmonious actions will add up and your character will be more than it ever was.

Character is the totality of your actions, thinking, omissions, and energy. If you are building character and momentum in your mind and world, other people and the Universe will instinctively know this. Therefore, your powers of attraction and usefulness to humanity will be appreciated, valued, and utilized.

With your energy in the now and your consciousness directed and pointed at *growth*, you will begin to flow effortlessly with life. Provided that you maintain a sense of peace and wholeness, you will maintain a connection to the universal power. In sum, your will can fuse and be energized by the true guidance of the world.

The Science of Gratitude in Twenty-Five Parts

1.   You believe that there is one intelligent substance from which all things proceed. Second, you believe that this substance gives you everything you desire. And third, you relate yourself to it by a feeling of deep and profound gratitude.

2.   The world is overflowing with good things, because life is in touch with the limitless source of all good things, and there is so much of everything that the wish of every heart can be gratified.

3.   We do not have to take from another to have abundance, because there is more than sufficient for all. The fact that some one has abundance does not prove that he has taken some or all of his wealth from others, although this is what a great many believe to be the truth.

4.   Whenever we see someone in luxury we wonder where and how he got it, and we usually add that many are in poverty because this one is in wealth. Such a doctrine, however, is not true. It is thoroughly false from beginning to end. The world is not so poverty stricken that the few cannot have plenty without stealing from the many.

5.   God is rich; the Universe is overflowing with abundance. If we have not everything that we want, there is a reason; there is some definite cause somewhere, either in ourselves or in our relations to the world, but this cause can be found and corrected; then we may proceed to take possession of our own.

6.   Among the many causes of poverty and the lack of a full supply there is one that has been entirely overlooked. To overcome this cause is to find one of the most important paths to perpetual increase, and the remedy lies within easy reach of everyone who has awakened to a degree the finer elements in their life.

7.   There may be exceptions to the rule, but there are thousands who are living on the husks of existence because they were not grateful when the kernels were received. Multitudes continue in poverty from no other cause than a lack of gratitude, and other thousands who have almost everything that the heart may wish for do not reach the coveted goal of full supply *because their gratitude is not complete.*

8.   If it is a New Thought to you that gratitude brings your whole mind into closer harmony with the creative energies of the Universe, consider it well, and you will see that it is true. Having received one gift from God, they cut the wires that connect them with him by failing to make acknowledgment.

9.   The grateful outreaching of your mind in thankful praise to the supreme intelligence is a liberation or expenditure of force. It cannot fail to reach that to which it addressed, and the reaction is an instantaneous movement toward you.

10. We are now beginning to realize more and more that the greatest thing in the world is to live so closely to the Infinite that we constantly feel the power and the peace of His presence. But the value of gratitude does not consist solely in getting you more blessings in the future. Without gratitude you cannot long keep from dissatisfied thought regarding things as they are.

11. In fact, this mode of living is the very secret of secrets revealing everything that the mind may wish to know or understand in order to make life what it is intended to be. We also realize that the more closely we live to the Infinite the more we shall receive of all good things, because all good things have their source in the Supreme; but how to enter into this life of supreme oneness with the Most High is a problem.

12. There are many things to be done in order to solve this problem, but there is no one thing that is more important in producing the required solution than deep, whole-souled gratitude. The soul that is always grateful lives nearer the true, the good, the beautiful and the perfect than anyone else in existence, and the more closely we live to the good and the beautiful the more we shall receive of all those things. The mind that dwells constantly in the presence of true worth is daily adding to its own worth. It is gradually and steadily appropriating that worth with which it is in constant contact; but we cannot enter into the real presence of true worth unless we fully appreciate the real worth of true worth; and all appreciation is based upon gratitude.

13. The grateful mind is constantly fixed upon the best. Therefore it tends to become the best. It takes the form or character of the best, and will receive the best. Also, faith is born of gratitude. The grateful mind continually expects good things, and expectation becomes faith. The reaction of gratitude upon one's own mind produces faith, and every outgoing wave of grateful thanksgiving increases faith.

14. Notice the grateful attitude that Jesus took, how he always seems to be saying, "I thank thee, Father, that thou hearest me." You cannot exercise much power without gratitude, for it is gratitude that keeps you connected with power.

15. The more grateful we are for the good things that come to us now the more good things we shall receive in the future. This is a great metaphysical law, and we shall find it most profitable to comply exactly with this law, no matter what the circumstances may be. Be grateful for everything and you will constantly receive more of everything; thus the simple act of being grateful becomes a path to perpetual increase. The reason is that the mental attitude of real gratitude will draw you in much closer contact with that power that produces the good things received.

16. In other words, to be grateful for what we have received is to draw more closely to the source of that which we receive. The good things that come to us come because we have properly employed certain laws, and when we are grateful for the results gained we enter into more perfect harmony with those laws and thus become able to employ those laws to still greater advantage in the immediate future. This anyone can understand, and those who do not know that gratitude produces this effect should try it and watch results.

17. The attitude of gratitude brings the whole mind into more perfect and more harmonious relations with all the laws and powers of life. The grateful mind gains a firmer hold, so to speak, upon those things in life that can produce increase. This is simply illustrated in personal experience where we find that we always feel nearer to that person to whom we express real gratitude. When you thank a person and truly mean it with heart and soul you feel nearer to that person than you ever did before. Likewise, when we express whole-souled thanksgiving to everything and everybody for everything that comes into life we draw closer and closer to all the elements and powers of life.

18. The moment you permit your mind to dwell with dissatisfaction upon things as they are, you begin to lose ground. You fix attention upon the common, the ordinary, the poor, the squalid, and the mean, and your mind takes away your power and you become distracted. The person who has no feeling of gratitude cannot long retain a living faith.

19. In other words, we draw closer to the real source from which all good things in life proceed. When we consider this principle from another point of view we find that the act of being grateful is an absolute necessity, if we wish to accomplish as much as we have the power to accomplish. To be grateful in this large, universal sense is to enter into harmony and contact with the greatest, the highest, and the best in life. We thus gain possession of the superior elements of mind and soul, and, in consequence, gain the power to become more and achieve more, no matter what our object or work may be. Everything that will place us in a more perfect relation with life, and thus enable us to appropriate the greater richness of life, should be employed with the greatest of earnestness, and deep whole-souled gratitude does possess a marvelous power in this respect. Its great value, however, is not confined to the laws just mentioned. Its power is exceptional in another and equally important field.

20. To be grateful is to think of the best, therefore the grateful mind keeps the eye constantly upon the best; and, according to another metaphysical law, we grow into the likeness of that which we think of the most. The mind that is always dissatisfied fixes attention upon the common, the ordinary, and the inferior, and thus grows into the likeness of those things. The creative forces within us are constantly making us just like those things upon which we habitually concentrate attention. Therefore, to mentally dwell upon the inferior is to become inferior, while to keep the eye single upon the best is to daily become better. The grateful mind is constantly looking for the best, thus holding attention upon the best and daily growing into the likeness of the best. The grateful mind expects only good things, and will always secure good things out of everything that comes. What we constantly expect we receive, and when we constantly expect to get good out of everything we cause everything to produce good.

21. Therefore, to the grateful mind all things will at all times work together for good, and this means perpetual increase in everything that can add to the happiness and the welfare of man. This being true, and anyone can prove it to be true, the proper course to pursue is to cultivate the habit of being grateful for everything that comes.

22. Give thanks eternally to the Most High for everything and feel deeply grateful every moment to every living creature. All things are so situated that they can be of some service to us, and all things have somewhere at some time been instrumental in adding to our welfare.

23. We must therefore, to be just and true, express perpetual gratitude to everything that has existence. Be thankful to yourself. Be thankful to every soul in the world, and most of all be thankful to the Creator of all that is. Live in perpetual thanksgiving to all the world, and express the deepest, sincerest, most whole-souled gratitude you can feel within whenever something of value comes into your life. When other things come, pass them by; never mind them in the least.

24. You know that the good in greater and greater abundance is eternally coming into your life, and for this give thanks with rejoicing; you know that every wish of the heart is being supplied; be thankful that this is true, and you will draw nearer and nearer to that place in life where what can be realized that you know is on the way to realization. Live according to this principle for a brief period of time, and the result will be that your life will change for the better to such a degree that you will feel infinitely more grateful than you ever felt before.

25. You will then find that thanksgiving and a grateful heart are necessary parts of real living, and you will also find that the more grateful you are for every ideal that has been made real, the more power you gain to press on to those greater heights where you will find every ideal to be real. And when this realization begins you are on the path to perpetual increase, because the more you receive the more grateful you feel, and the more grateful you feel for that which has been received the more closely you will live to that Source that can give you more.

These twenty-five parts were compiled, prepared, and extracted from the teachings and publications of Wallace D. Wattles, Christian D. Larson, Thomas Troward, Charles Haanel, and Edward Beals. These twenty-five elements of gratitude and abundance have been compiled and enhanced by Prof. Mentz. All of these authors published their philosophies that were used herein before 1920. * Please understand that anything that you praise, bless, thank, appreciate, or express gratitude towards, will be drawn to you.

Lord's Prayer & Other Daily Prayers

The applied psychology of daily prayer is misunderstood and even feared by many people. However, some best-selling books such as the "Sermon on the Mount" by Emmet Fox or "Prayer of Jabez," extracted a prayer of thanksgiving and protection from scripture to illuminate the lasting effect upon attitude, consciousness, and Spirit.

In these books, it is uncanny how this little prayer from ancient scripture can be difficult for people to understand, master or even use. These prayers are asking for protection and expansion, and offer praise. Asking for help and blessings is sometimes an act that many persons have never done unless sheer danger or peril was near. Some have never had a personal God or cooperative universe to offer praise to, request protection, petition for blessings, or ask for an expanded role in doing good works. After further examination and trial, these types of prayers are very liberating because they seem to bring you closer to peace and abundance in a very rapid way.

This holds true for the Lord's Prayer where this prayer asks for daily blessings, protection from trespasses, along with the ability to forgive. Overall, when you thank or praise the Universe or God for blessings while asking for help, it seems to open the flood gates of more and more blessings into your life. Furthermore, it also opens the door to serve humanity also.

Thoughts Are Things by Prentice Mulford – Summary
13 Chapter Summaries Analyzed from the 1908 Book
Revisions and commentary by Prof. Mentz

Chapter One is focusing on the cooperation of the self with Spirit. If we as students of metaphysics realize that a harmonious relationship with our inner self and higher self is a relationship of peace and success, then our cooperation will allow a fusion with our Spiritual and material life. It is an inside job, and we must clear ourselves on the inside to make for the great good and peace that can fill ourselves and our souls with constructive Spirit energy.

Chapter Two is concerned with our external environment and our Spiritual and physical associations. If we associate with like minds of Spiritual nature, we can excel. Persons who encourage and support our growth are good for our growth and health. Many authors throughout history have advocated researching those whom we admire. Ask for their insight. Learn to be the best by associating with the best. Put yourself in the company of those who are constructive. Act as if you are your ideal. Learn to reinvent yourself and grow toward your desired character and image. Avoid those persons who are destructive. Engage life, stay active, help others, and they will help you.

Chapter Three: Thoughts are things. We think, therefore, we are. We are beings of thoughts and creations. What you think is emitted and sent out from you. Your thoughts attract like thoughts. Through constructive thinking, focus, concentration, action, gratitude, thanksgiving, and praise, these things will be brought back to you. Be very specific in your petitions and desires. You are a magnet for higher good if you project good.

Chapter Four: The courage to think what you want and to take action towards what you want is an ultimate power. This type of control and focus may allow you to see in your mind's eye what it is you want and will do. This type of visualization and mental planning prepares you for each day's actions and work. In the present moment, we can do all we can toward our objectives. We cannot change yesterday or do tomorrow's work. We must use our mind and actions toward today's goals and mission.

Chapter Five: This chapter is dealing with the effective use of our Spiritual and emotional energy. If we live in the past and dwell on what has been wrong in our life, then our present energy is dissipated in favor of the ills of the past. Do not blame your past for anything. You are capable of all things new. Your body and mind can be renewed altogether with continued Spiritual and metaphysical focus. Our emotions are very important. If we use our present days, present thoughts, and visualization toward our desired ideals and mix this with our constructive emotion; then, we can move quickly toward what we want from life. Moreover, we can sometimes move effortlessly towards our True Place in conjunction with the will of our Higher Power. As Mulford states, prolonged grief and self-sabotage can destroy our growth and body. Additionally, resentments, anger, hatred, and self-loathing will indeed attract more of the same into your life. Severing from the past, asking for forgiveness, making amends, doing a self-appraisal and proper atonement if possible will free your mind from self-tyranny.

Chapter Six: Mulford states, "We get the element of love only in proportion as we have it in us." Thus, love is the quality of thought and emotion that will propel us into "peace of mind" and also great success. Love all there is. Focus on the good, the best, the constructive, and the beauty of life. See the best in all there is. See the good that results from the world. Meditate on the people that have been good to you, the creation all around you, the good that happens every day, the inventions for the good of humanity, and the positive happenings around the world that occur each and every day. Learn to love all and love yourself, and love will be attracted to you.

Love is a form of gratitude, harmlessness, peace, kindness, and care. Thinking love and giving love will liberate you into the forth dimension of thought. Think of how you have been blessed, protected, and guided throughout your life. Yes, lessons have been learned, and further happiness, peace, and success may be yours if you stay on the path of Spiritual abundance.

Chapter Seven: Mulford states, "If you in your mind are ever building an ideal of yourself as strong, healthy, and vigorous, you are building to yourself of invisible element that which is ever drawing to you more of health, strength, and vigor." With this being said, thoughts of greater things, thoughts of health, thoughts of harmonious relationships, thoughts of peace, and thoughts of wealth will project into the world and mould your life. Further, people will be attracted to you to add to and increase your world and journey. Health, beauty, confidence, and success are mostly a state of mind. We have all seen an average-looking superstar be regarded as absolutely beautiful. Thus, how we think and carry ourselves most definitely affects how we are perceived and how we feel day-to-day.

Chapter Eight: As you know, freedom is important. Allowing ourselves to engage life while heading towards our true place and right livelihood is fundamentally important. People who relegate themselves to something that they do not want to do for their lifetime may be inhibiting their happiness and their potential service to humanity. As with the birds and other animals, each person must seek out what he or she wants from life. Nobody is stopping you from following your dreams. We are not animals. We have choices and an abundance of opportunity in this world. Ask yourself what you want to be, who you want to be with, and how and where you want to live. Think about the possibilities. Coalesce the choices of jobs, careers, business ventures, and creative alternatives that you have in your present and future. Imagine what a person in jail is limited to. Then, envision all of the great gifts and prospects that you have in your life.

The Secrets Decoded

Chapter Nine: Mulford states that, "All things" are possible with God. "God works in and through you." We are all parts of the Infinite Power, a power ever carrying us up to higher, finer, happier grades of being. Good is on your side. God is your partner in life. If you join forces through cooperation and contemplation of your Higher Spirit, then you will believe that only good is possible and faith will be induced through your harmonious and thankful mind set and action. As Mulford suggests, "Christ's Spirit or thought had power to command the elements, and quiet the storm. Your Spirit as a part of the great whole has in it the germ, and the same power is waiting for fruition within you. Christ, through power of concentrating the unseen element of his thought, could turn that unseen element into the seen, and materialize food--loaves and fishes." Never underestimate yourself, never speak with discouragement to others, do not keep the habit of doubting opportunity and good. The word "impossible" may be completely untrue. Impossible is a simple response to what others have forced you to believe. Impossible is a simple-minded response and excuse to doing anything. Rather ask: Why not?

Chapter Ten: In this chapter, Mulford is directing us to the reality of the body and its capabilities. The body can grow, heal, renew, learn, and do great works. However, we must realize that rest and peace are vitally important to this growth and renewal. The body or temple is renewing itself daily with new cells and cleansing itself of the old. When we permit our body and soul to grow, heal, and regenerate, we become more effective each day. Christ said, "Ask, and ye shall receive: seek, and ye shall find, knock, and it shall be opened unto you." What this means is that we can ask in our mind, seek and find what we desire. The kingdom is working with us at every moment to help produce what we need. We should only cooperate with the Higher Power with clarity, thanks, and gratitude to allow these things to be given. We must be ready to receive the gifts of the Spirit in the highest form. We would be wise to allow the gift to be given and have an open mind and heart to the ideal that comes to us.

Chapter Eleven: "Thy faith hath made thee whole," said the Christ of Judea to a man who was healed." Are you ready for a better life? Do you believe that all things good are possible? Can your thinking and your character be transformed toward higher thought and toward constructive thinking of Spiritual abundance? In this chapter, a "childlike faith" is mentioned. If we were to approach things as if they are possible, then would we have a better chance of success and happiness? Become open to that inflowing force of Spirit and abundance. Allow yourself to change for the better, take action, and move forward toward your highest good.

Chapter Twelve: Begin your day with taming your mind with Spiritual and constructive thoughts. Feed your body, mind, and soul with the best food, information, and Spiritual energy. Act, think, and be good to yourself and others. Ask and petition from your higher power all that you want. Hope and pray for the best to happen to all and everyone. Bless, praise, and be thankful for all things good. Empower yourself and your Spirit with love, gratitude, kindness, harmonious thinking, harmless action, and serenity. Your highest ideals will be provided by the Universe as long as you do not resist the gifts of abundance and are contemplative in action.

Chapter Thirteen: New thinking is possible. It is a simple adjustment to the way we use our mind. Try to *not* complain for a one whole day. Try to stop blaming. Quit making excuses for not doing what you desire. Your thoughts and character can be reinvented. You can be reborn. Your mind and thinking can transcend into a new constructive awareness. It takes time and effort, but anyone can do it. We must be persistent. In life or business we must press on in mind to achieve the successful results that we desire. Each day is a new opportunity to engage several successful tasks. We need not act in haste.

Conclusion: We can perform tasks effectively and efficiently toward our ideals and goals. We must see in mind or imagination the thing we plan in its completed form, the system or method organized and in working order, the movement or undertaking advancing and ever growing stronger, constructive, and more profitable. To spend time and force in looking back and living past troubles or obstacles over again, and out of such living and mental action to conjure more difficulties or oppositions, is literally to spend time and force in destroying your undertaking, or in manufacturing obstacles to put in your own way.

There is no need to speak or think of the past. The past has taught us lessons. We may not have achieved what we wanted or have been treated fairly. However, we have learned a lesson and need never to participate in a destructive engagement again. Risks we must take, but our new risks will be calculated because we will be prepared for anything that comes our way. We can avoid certain things and engage healthy ones. All experiences are valuable for the wisdom they bring or suggest. But when you have once gained wisdom and knowledge from any experience, there is little profit in repeating it, especially if it has been unpleasant,

Our thought is the unseen magnet, ever attracting its correspondence in things seen and tangible. As we realize this more and more clearly, we shall become more and more careful to keep our minds set in the right direction on self-improvement. It is our divine right to have a rich and full life with Spiritual abundance. The Universe will send people to help us and guide us. We will accept their help and create win-win relationships where all benefit. What is important to you. You Spiritual and material life should both be important to you. What you make important to you will grow. If you make your family, your success, and your wealth important, all will grow in your life. When you blend your visionary mind, your emotion, your thoughts, and your action toward what you want, you will indeed meet your goals and dreams, particularly if you maintain a harmonious and grateful relationship with your Higher Power.

Continue to make prayers and petitions to your higher self or God. See in your mind's eye what you truly want. Do not be afraid to ask for anything that is good for you and for all. Hold that picture of completed success in your mind. Project it on the picture screen of your mind with sharp and defined clarity. Claim it as yours and thank your higher self and higher power for providing it to you. Be thankful, affirm your blessings, and take action toward what you want. Send it out of your mind into the world with thanks and confident expectation knowing that the thing you desire or something better will come into your life or unfold in your life's journey.

Robert Collier: 25 Secrets to Spiritual Achievement:

1. Collier believed that the great kingdom was within and ready to be tapped if you chose to do so.
2. He quoted the masters in saying that we should live life abundantly.
3. He clearly shows through simple truths that mankind has repeatedly denied possibilities and miracles to be proven wrong shortly thereafter. Examples: Flight, space travel, impersonal uses of electricity.
4. He suggests that we come from the great Intelligence, and where there is intelligence, there is responsiveness.
5. Where there is responsiveness, there is the ability to cooperate and co-create our destiny.
6. The greatest methods of creating responsiveness are to use: praise, blessing, gratitude, and love. Direct these forces coupled with faith toward the desired objectives.
7. He advocated that whatever we focused on with harmonious, thankful, loving, and grateful thoughts would be expanded into our life.
8. All of these forces of love, blessing, and gratitude, and such are energies of emotion. Constructive and positive emotion blended with specific desire creates great power.
9. He brings up the secrets of Philippians IV, and states that if we make petitions to the Universe with harmonious thoughts and emotions, our prayers would be answered or unfold during our life.
10. Sincere desire is necessary to manifest anything on the Spiritual and physical plane. Single-mindedness of purpose and thought is needed to fuel the actualization of your desires.
11. One of Collier's favorite topics is the issue of the power of attraction or "Like attracts like." Thus, like energy attracts similar energy of that vibration.
12. He discusses relaxation techniques to better commune with the Great Spirit of Abundance.

13. Collier in some writings discusses the poetry of von Goethe. Von Goethe's famous poem states, "Boldness is genius." As such, Collier believes that each idea/action does in fact start a momentum of activity or energy toward any objective.

14. Thus, action must be engaged, one thing at a time. Work effectively without haste and do things right the first time if possible.

15. Collier also had respect for the axiom, "Believe that Ye Receive Them." The secret of claiming something in mind before you have it. Collier and many other authors sanction the use of affirmations spoken aloud or silently to convince your inner-self or subconscious of the opportunity and fact of having the thing as real.

16. Overall, Collier emphasized that having gratitude for something before you receive it is the secret catalyst to Spiritual manifesting.

17. He implies never to talk or speak against yourself or in a negative way in public or mentally.

18. Collier completely believes in the use of mental images and visualization as a tool of manifesting your desires. Thus, this law of manifestation allows us to call into our outer world whatever we truly believe in our inner world. See things as you would have them in a very specific form.

19. We can only obtain what we think we can have.

20. With regard to poverty, Collier understood that it was a disease, contagious, and causes great and unnecessary harm. Moreover, anyone who teaches people to be unworthy of excellence and abundance does great harm to the masses. This point usually was made to exclaim the unlimited supply of the earth and Universe.

21. Collier would also point out Einstein's law as a way to explain that there is only one material in the Universe, e.g., energy.

22. Collier believed that the mind was part of the universal energy and receives abundance from it. Moreover, he believed that ideas were things much like thoughts are things. Ideas should be considered and cultivated and acted upon or set in motion.

23. With anything you want, you furnish the mental idea and energy of it in mind. Hold it in your mind's eye. This desire will act like a magnet to what is needed for it to materialize over time. The stronger the desires and actions towards a harmonious and constructive objective, the quicker the forces necessary will be drawn to you.

24. As with all else, *believe in yourself*, believe you are worthy, and be willing to receive the great things in life.

25. After you have honed any good idea, do things to bring it to life.

Note on Robert Collier:

Through Mr. Collier's studies of applied metaphysics and mind sciences, he implies that things grow in our life by expansion. He refers to the biblical word "kingdom," i.e., "Seek the Kingdom first," as the Greek word for "expansion." Therefore, if we seek, direct, and utilize expansion it will multiply in our mind and life. Whatever is praised and blessed multiplies in our life. Overall, love is the most powerful form of expanding force. Hence, when love, praise, blessings and such are directed anywhere, life will multiply where the energy is directed. He quotes Philippians IV in this lesson also. See Philippians in the Glossary. "Rejoice, Be Glad, Give Thanks." In Collier's 1925 7 Volume version of "The Book of Life", Robert Collier addresses many of these concepts. On page 38, it says, " Man is an active part of this Universal Mind. That he partakes of its creative wisdom and power and that by working in harmony with Universal Mind he can do anything, have anything, be anything."

George Mentz, JD, MBA

An Analysis of the Secrets of Judge Thomas Troward.

Judge Thomas Troward – The Edinburg Lectures

Judge Troward worked in India in the 1800's. His codification or world teachings influenced many of the greatest thinkers of the twentieth century American self-help movement. Troward believed that the world was Universal Mind, and the seed of all things is thought in conjunction with the universal source. To materialize anything, one must think it and develop sufficient desire for the goal, coupled with a clear mental image of the outcome.

Further, Troward emphasized developing oneness with the source of all or Universal Mind. As he once stated, "Matter is not an illusion but a necessary channel through which life differentiates energy." Moreover, "The raw material for the formation of the solar systems is universally distributed throughout all space. This raw material can be cultivated by our mental and Spiritual powers." Thus, our mental pictures are the "attraction energy" that allows original substance to take shape. Your mental pictures, constructive thoughts, and concentration mixed with your "I-am-ness" or "harmonious relationship with the Universal Mind" is the recipe that can allow success.

Troward refers to the Invisible Supply in the same way as Universal Mind. He suggests meditation or quite reflection several times per day or (morning and night time). Other exercises may include relaxation or allowing a mental circle of light to surround you and bless you. Develop one-ness and harmony with the Source of All. Then, you can go over your mental pictures of what you want. Quiet and relaxed contemplation along with visualization and confident action is the desired equation for effective meditation.

Steps in Troward's Cosmic Manifestation Process

- Relax and cultivate oneness with the Universal Mind or Source of All. (Recognize that you are part of all and in communion with all.)
- Specify exactly what conditions you desire to produce.
- Specify in your mind what you will do with the results of the desire.
- Concentrate the thoughts on the mental picture.
- Visualize the possibilities with confident expectation.
- There is no need to strain. Peacefully allow your thoughts and visualizations to be pictured in the highest outcome.
- Do your visualizations with a grateful frame of mind.
- Your mental images are specific, but you should be open to results that are even better than you have specified.
- Mentally become open to receive and have the desired condition or result.
- Accept that the condition can be yours and believe that you *have it*.
- After this, go out into the world with your intuition and plans and *take action*, leaving no stone unturned.
- Affirmations can influence your belief. An example is the following: Repeating the word "joy" with emotion and with persistence can allow you to live and feel joy.
- Approaching your goals, actions, and mental exercises with enthusiasm and a thankful heart can be a catalyst to your desires.

Judge Troward - The Hidden Powers of Abundance

Truth:

Truth is generally defined by your individual perception by affected by many external variables along with being tilted by your preconceptions. Therefore, every truth may have something beyond what is apparent. The constant influx of perceptions blended with your views and opinions and race mind tend to make it difficult for harmonious thinking as well as a harmonious relationship of your energies with the Universe. With the exercise and mastering of the mind and thoughts, a person's inner and Spiritual conditions can be enhanced dramatically for the good.

Many would say that we are in a dream state and living in illusion until we get out of our state of being self-absorbed and connect to the source of all on a Spiritual level. As the Universe is governed by many laws including the "Law of Growth," change occurs rapidly and we must adapt and grow on a Spiritual and mental level to cooperate with the Universe. When we grow and heal from the inside, we can become much stronger, wiser, and more at peace.

Unity:

It is well known that Spiritual freedom and abundance can be greatly enhanced through unity with all. We can develop and achieve this type of unity by cultivating the following: praise, love, gratitude, and blessings toward our inner Christ and outward God. *If* the Kingdom of Heaven is truly everywhere and within us, then, it was Jesus who stated that we must put this relationship *first* to achieve everlasting life. Further, Spirit and matter are equally important and of the same energy. Thus, we must learn to co-create our life by building this force within us. As with quantum physics, all is energy and the Spiritual mind has the ability to energize and make alive that same matter-building energy.

Responsiveness of Spirit:

Spirit is also responsive and personal in nature. The relationship to the Spiritual forces and energies can only be developed by ourselves and no one can do it for us.

If this relationship that we have with Spirit is sour, then it is contingent upon our efforts to harmonize it. When harmonized, the relationship is more responsive. The Spirit has a tendency to add increase and good into our lives if we are connected to it. If not, then that energy becomes dormant.

When we awaken the possibilities of life and activate our focus on the source through cooperation, then a new dimension of thinking and acting will become available.

ASK:

We are manifestations of the Spirit; thus, we come from the very source that we call upon. The Universe is unlimited and abundant and awaits our requests and relationship.

A Spiritual demand does in fact create supply from nothingness, and this supply may be freely applied to any and every subject matter within our sphere of availability. The power or Spirit or universal energy is characterized by love, and to give it love is to facilitate love from the very source of creation.

The " I AM", Thought and Character

The word "I AM" is most important because I am what I am *and* I may be what I will to be. My individuality is one of the modes in which the Infinite expresses itself, and therefore I am myself that very power that I find to be the innermost within of all things. To attain true power is to free yourself of "destructive mind" activity and thinking. We may never be totally free, but reducing the thinking and self-defeating mind conversations will be a great start. Give yourself a break and do not beat-up on yourself so much. If you begin to think in terms of *good* and ideal circumstances and opportunity, *then*, opportunities will unfold. Constructive and spiritual thoughts are a hundred times more powerful than negative ones. However, if you think a hundred negative thoughts to every one excellent thought, then you are paralyzed being left with nothing. What we mean to say is this: If you can allow constructive thoughts to become natural thought to you, then you will advance and grow very quickly in a short period of time provided you maintain this ability. Because you feel that you are; thus, you feel the "I AM". The "I AM" is your essence and your connectedness to the infinate all.

The Past:

We are byproducts of intelligence and love, which rule the Universe. However, our mind and body are temples that contain what we choose to harvest. In essence, we must purge our minds of the destructive past. Sometimes this may take great work and discussions with a Spiritual advisor or therapist. The goal is not to refocus on the past, but to let it go. We must realize that the past *cannot* drive our future and *we must* not allow the past to be an excuse to stop growing and living. Through self-analysis, constructive living, meditation, and prayer, we can make ourselves open to receive all the good that is available to us.

We must clean out our self-defeating thoughts of the past to make room for the good. Within a short period, we can re-fill our Spirit minds with a pure and strong energy that can only re-vitalize our souls and connection with Spiritual abundance.

Forgiveness:

Forgiveness and atonement may be one of the most fundamental paths to freedom and strength. If we can overcome anger, resentment, and the past, we become very powerful indeed. This mental freedom affords us the very abilities that we crave: of love, gratitude, focus, concentration, and bold action.

What is important about harmony and peace of mind is that they afford us the protection against the forces of confusion and anxiety. By forming a bond with the Creator, we can be protected from losing our awareness of good and be guided to avoid discouragement. By keeping our guard and maintaining ourselves on a Spiritual level, we are tapped in the unlimited power of abundance.

Unlimited Abundance:

Understanding our inner Spirit in relation to the Higher Spirit is critical. Developing unity to it is also key. As we advance in this knowledge, we know ourselves to be unlimited, and that, in the miniature world, whose center we are, we ourselves are the very same overflowing of joyous livingness that the Great Life Spirit is in the Great All. The I AM is One. Thus, we exist in correlation to the larger Force with whom we can successfully cooperate.

Prayer, self-analysis, gratitude, and meditation can form the nexus with our Supreme Power as we understand it. This is the meaning of prayer. Prayer is not a foolish seeking to change the mind of Supreme Wisdom, but it is an intelligent seeking to embody that wisdom in our thoughts so as more and more perfectly to express *it* in expressing *ourselves*. Thus, as we gradually grow into the habit of finding this inspiring Presence *within ourselves.*

Your Purpose:

Practicing control over our thoughts is an exercise that can grant us freedom from anxiety and discouragement. Therefore think life, illumination, harmony, prosperity, and happiness. Use the powers of self-affirmation vocally and in silence to strengthen and redirect your subconscious mind power toward ideals and objectives that will grow and increase your life.

Decide what you want your mind and Spirit to hold and be filled with. Determine *now* that you will assert your power towards thoughts and ideas of success, happiness, health, and service. Take control of your mind and life as you know it. By revitalizing your thinking, you may reinvent yourself and be reborn into a new dimension of living.

Submission and Cooperation:

The Supreme Power wants nothing of war, illness, disease, or suffering. There is an unlimited supply of good on this earth. Troward implies that we make submission. Submission to what? What he is saying is to put your Spirit before your ego mind. Cooperate with both energies and powers. Your inner Spirit and higher power are one in the same. If you are in tune with the inner forces, you have effectively made submission to them in the form of thankful and constructive humility. Through this unseen joint venture, the two powers of ego and Spirit become unified into a powerful force for self-good and self-actualization.

Recognition:

The awakening to consciousness is a desire to be led by the will of our inner and higher powers. If we cultivate a willingness to cultivate the ideas of our higher self, then we can act upon what is recognized and realized. Everything depends on our recognition. Thoughts are things, and therefore as we *will* our thoughts to be, so we also *will* the thing to be.

The Great Within:

The powers you seek are within. You need only to tap into them. Many people do not understand their wholeness and completeness under the Supreme Powers. We need not try to affect others, we must focus within. We can grow and increase within and also regenerate our minds from within. When we begin to master and understanding of our wholeness and ability to connect to the Supreme Powers, we then can improve our thinking, harmony with all, and our effective actions on this material and physical plane. Change and improvement from within is the *key*. Others are not responsible for our character. Our character is the totality of our thinking and actions, and we can reinvent our character according to our needs and dreams. Remember, the body and cells are replaced every few months. Thus, our body, cells, and sub-atomic nature can be replaced with higher properties and energies.

Desire:

Desire is *good*. Desire drives us to improve, adapt, and better our life for our family and ourselves. Desire is much like creation and self-preservation. The desires come from Universal Mind. The ideas and desires are provided to us to save ourselves from destruction along with advancing ourselves inwardly and outwardly. Desires would not exist if they were not possible in mind and on the physical plane. Sometimes we must act to grow and persevere. Specific and clear desires create very powerful thought energy. Constructive and creative desires that are harmless in nature are extremely powerful. Cause and effect are mathematically pure. If we continue to think and do things in a certain way toward an objective, we create a cause that the Universe works with us to create the effect in an equal of higher form. Your desire is intuitive and within you. Sometimes you must act toward your constructive and expansive desires to meet your inner self half-way. Therefore, it is vital for growth and peace of mind to sometimes follow your dreams, cultivate thought, and take action.

Mastering Thought:

Thoughts, events, and things are at our disposal. We should understand that things are for our use and mastery. If they are not useful, then we may not need them. However, we must all be able to act without haste or worry. We must be able to master circumstances and take control of our tasks, objectives, and goals.

Know Thyself:

Truth can set us free. Know thyself and you can conquer self-defeating thoughts. We can *think* what we please, and if to think is to form, then we can form what we please. Man himself is therefore a mode of the divine thought. Again, man is self-conscious; therefore man is the divine thought evolved into *individual* consciousness, and when he becomes sufficiently enlightened to realize this as his origin, then he sees that he is a reproduction *in individuality* of the *same* Spirit that produces all things. Let us, then, confidently claim our birthright as sons and daughters of the Almighty, and by habitually thinking the good, the beautiful, and the true, surround ourselves with conditions corresponding to our thoughts, and by our teaching and example help others to do the same.

Bold Action and Livelihood:

Actions need not be done in anxiety or haste, but we do them well with constructive passion toward the fulfillment of the will that guides us. As our desires and ideas are in tune with our inner self, we act in accordance with our dreams. Thus, the labor will be a joyful experience. The essence of this action is *right livelihood*. When cooperating with mind, ego, people sent to help us, and the physical world, living and working becomes fun and invigorating. You see, our true place and true career become self-evident through the evolution and use of these practices in our life. When we are operating within the sphere of our destiny, joy and beauty becomes obvious and our work becomes much more effortless and strong.

Preemptive Strike:

The religion, politics and creed of others is not of our concern. The beliefs of the masses should not affect our growth or abundance. If we focus on our purpose and ideals with mental clarity, we have a clear advantage. Many of us and others have habits, philosophy, and religions that are of good use. Thus, there is no need to speak or think against anyone. Wish all people well. Bless all people. Recognize and praise greatness and excellence. Any practice that enables a person to realize unity with Divine Spirit and truth is good. If we act and think in ways that show others of our worth, goodness, and kindness, then we all stand to benefit through the laws of attraction. Think the best, be the best, and give your best toward your true destiny.

Inner and Outer:

As above, so below. The inner workings of our mind and body are extremely important. However, we should understand that the outer world must be analyzed. If the outer shows certain signs and symbols, then we have the opportunity to improve our inner world so as to advance our outer.

Spiritual Flow and Opulence:

If we clearly realize that the creative power in ourselves is *unlimited*, then there is no reason for limiting the extent to which we may enjoy what we can create by means of it. Where we are drawing from the *infinite* we need never be afraid of taking more than our share. Giving can only increase your life and the Spiritual flow into it. Giving without expectation creates a vacuum of which you must be rewarded in due form. There are other sorts of wealth that are truly valuable both on the Spiritual and intellectual planes, which you can give; and you can start from this point and practice the Spirit of opulence, even though your balance at the bank may be nil. If you have realized the *Spirit* of opulence you *cannot help* drawing to yourself material good, as well as that higher wealth that is not to be measured by a money standard.

Wealth will be yours thought your thoughts, ideals, gratitude, action, service, and giving. The essence of any desire must be determined. How are you going to use the wealth, and how will you serve your family, charity, or humanity with it? How much are you going to *do* by it? It is not money, but the *love* of money, that is the root of evil; and the *Spirit* of opulence is precisely the attitude of mind that is furthest removed from the love of money for its own sake. We are not called upon to give what we have not yet received and to run into debt; but we are to give liberally of what we have, with the knowledge that by so doing we are setting the law of circulation to work, and as this law brings us greater and greater inflows of every kind of good, so our out-giving will increase, not by depriving ourselves of any expansion of our own life that we may desire, but by finding that every expansion makes us the more powerful instruments for expanding the lives of others. Giving and tithing as if we are indeed blessed with unlimited wealth and abundance will begin and continue this reality in our life. We must identify ourselves with the *Spirit* of opulence. We must be opulent in our *thought*. Do not *think money*, as such, for it is only one means of opulence; but *think opulence*, that is, largely, generously, liberally, and you will find that the means of realizing this thought will flow to you from all quarters, whether as money or as a hundred other things not to be equated with just cash.

Beauty:

See beauty. Think beauty. Appreciate what is good. When your mind gets into the habit of this type of recognition, the beauty of the earth becomes part of you. Recognizing beauty will produce beauty for you. Truly seeing what is beautiful will allow you to cultivate harmonious thoughts of harmlessness. This type of thought draws the higher self to you. Appreciating beauty is a form of gratitude and love. Moreover, absorbing beauty will also allow you to absorb faith in the miracles of life. When we recognize the probabilities of true miracles, then they become *real* and *visible* to our thought.

"We cannot serve both God and mammon," says the Bible. There is no such thing as partial wholeness. Either we are still in the principle of separateness, and our eyes are not yet open to the real nature of the Kingdom of Heaven; or else we have grasped the principle of Unity without any exception anywhere, and the One Being includes all, the body and the soul alike, the visible form and the invisible substance and life of all equally. Nothing can be left out, and we stand complete here and now, lacking no faculty, but requiring only to become conscious of our own powers, and to learn to have confidence in them through having them exercised by reason of use.

Therefore, all is from God and there is *no* other force that need be recognized or dealt with. To have opposing powers is to allow duality in mind and Spirit.

One Force of Good:

Dualism can imply many things. If we put anything between our connection or unity to Divine Mind, then we are obstructing the channel and flow of power. Thus, opposing forces or thoughts can be anything that frustrates your conscious connection to Spirit. Examples can be in the form of discouragement, envy, pride, lust, obsession, anger, greed, gluttony, or sloth. A simple method of eliminating these types of thoughts are discussing them with a trusted advisor for the purposes of releasing their power over you. Or we may always begin to pray for another person to create our own mental harmony toward their Spirit.

Illusions:

Negativity and illness are not the true nature of anything. It is simply a lack of good. And because destructive forces are not in the true nature of the things themselves, nor yet in the Universal Mind, which is the Originating Principle, there remains only one place for it to spring from, and that is our own personal racing thought. We must refuse to know these confusing thoughts; we must refuse to admit that there is any such thing to be known. If we fear some rare disease and think about it all day, we give it power when in fact *it does not exist*. If we fear that another will say or do something to harm us, then we begin to act in a way that is in expectation of its manifestation.

Give *no* Spiritual energy to this type of ridiculous thought. You are a *perfect* and harmonious creation of God and Spirit that is constantly being renewed and revitalized. You are in harmony with yourself; thus, in harmony with the world. Therefore, the world will act to protect and guide you as you cooperate with spiritual abundance.

No Limits:

To enter into the Spirit of anything, then, is to make yourself one in thought with the creative principle that is at the centre of it. Therefore why not go to the centre of all things at once, and enter into the Spirit of Life? Do you ask where to find it? *In yourself*; and in proportion as you find it there, you will find it everywhere else. Look at Life as the one thing that is, whether in you or around you. Try to realize the livingness of it, and then seek to enter into the Spirit of it by affirming it to be the whole of what you are. Affirm this continually in your thoughts, and by degrees the affirmation will grow into a real living force within you, so that it will become a second nature to you, and you will find it impossible and unnatural to think in any other way. The nearer you approach this point the greater you will find your control over both body and circumstances, until at last you shall so enter into the Spirit of the divine creative power that is the root of all things-- that, in the words of Jesus, "nothing shall be impossible to you," because you have so entered into the Spirit of it that you discover yourself to be *one with it*. Then all the old limitations will have passed away and you will be living in an entirely new world of life, liberty, and love, of which you yourself are the radiating centre. You will realize the truth that your thought is a limitless creative power, and that you yourself are behind your thought, controlling and directing it with knowledge for any purpose that love motives and wisdom plans. Thus you will cease from your labors, struggles, and anxieties, and enter into that new order where perfect rest is one with ceaseless activity.

I Am what I Am:

The very essence of the teaching of the great master is this: Unbelief in the limitless power of life-in-ourselves--in each of us--is the one cause of death and of all those evils which, in greater or lesser measure, reproduce the restrictive influences which deprive life of its fullness and joy. If we would escape death and enter into life, we must each believe in the I AM in ourselves.

As for death, many people have their character die while they are alive, and they are then reborn. How is this done? By a shift in your path and sometimes by a catharsis of mind. Sometimes, this catharsis or cleansing is done operatively and speculatively with the help of another person. This person would allow you expose your faults, forgive yourself, and forgive others *permanently*. The I AM includes 'everything. It is at once "the Way, the Truth, and the Life": not the life only, or the Truth only, but also the way by which to reach them. Can words be more plain? It is by continually affirming and relying on the I AM in ourselves as identical with the I AM that is the one and only life, whether manifested or unmanifested, in all places of the Universe, that we shall find the way to the attainment of all truth and of all life. Here we have the predicate that we are seeking to complete our affirmation regarding ourselves. I AM--what? I AM the three things that include all things: Truth, which is all knowledge and wisdom; life, which is all power and love; and the unfailing way, which will lead us step by step. If we follow it, it will guide us to heights beyond what our present juvenile imagination is able to picture. This is the universal and eternal affirmation to which no predicate is attached. And all particular affirmations will be found to be only special differentiations of this all-embracing one. I will this or that particular thing because I know that I can bring it into externalization, and I know that I can because I know that I AM part of ALL, and so we always come back to the great central affirmation of all-being. Search the ancient scriptures of the world, and you will find that from first to last they teach only this: Every human soul is an individualization of that Universal Being, or All-Spirit, which we call God, and that Spirit can never be shorn of its powers, but like fire, which is its symbol, must always be fully and perfectly itself, which is life in all its unlimited fullness.

Giving Thanks:

St. John says, "This is the boldness that we have towards him, that if we ask anything according to His will, He heareth us; and if we know that He heareth us whatsoever we ask, we know that we have the petitions that we have asked of Him" (1 John v. 14).

Here, then, we find the secret of power. It is contained in the true worship of the Father, which is the constant recognition of the lifegivingness of Originating Spirit, and of the fact that we, as individuals, still continue to be portions of that Spirit, and that therefore the law of our nature is to be perpetually drawing life from the inexhaustible stores of the Infinite--not bottles of water-of-life mixed with other ingredients and labeled for this or that particular purpose, but the full flow of the pure stream itself, which we are free to use for any purpose we desire. "Whosoever will, let him take the water of life freely." It is thus that the worship of the Father becomes the central principle of the individual life, not as curtailing our liberty, but as affording the only possible basis for it. As a planetary system would be impossible without a central controlling sun, so harmonious life is impossible without the recognition of Infinite Spirit as that power, whose generic tendency serves to control each individual being into its proper orbit.

Divine Rights and Blessings:

All that hinders individuals from exercising the full power of the Infinite for any purpose whatever is their lack of faith, their inability to realize to the fullest, the stupendous truth that they themselves are the very power they seek. This was the teaching of Jesus as it is that of the New Thought; and this truth of the divine sonship of man should be realized by all who desire wholeness. Limitations exist only where we ourselves put them, and that to view ourselves as beings of limitless knowledge, power, and love is to become such in outward manifestation of visible fact.

As for effective prayer, the great master bids us believe that we have already in fact received what we ask for, and makes this the condition of receiving; in other words, he makes the essential factor in the mental action to consist in absolute certainty as to the corresponding response in the Infinite, which is exactly the condition that the historical masters lay down for the successful operation of thought power.

Conclusion

I conclude with a momentous question: What happens if we go counter to the law of Spirit? What happens if we go counter to any natural law? Obviously, the law goes counter to us. The law of Spirit, like all other natural laws, is in itself impersonal, but we carry into it, so to speak, the reflection of our own personality, though we cannot alter its character. Therefore, if we oppose its generic tendency towards the universal good and constructive or confident expectation of good, we shall find in it the reflection of our own opposition.

The law of Spirit proceeds unalterably on its course, and what is spoken of in popular phraseology as the divine wrath is nothing else than the reflex action that naturally follows when we put ourselves in opposition to this law. The non-good that results on this earthly plane is not a personal intervention of the Universal Spirit, but it is the natural outcome of the causes that we ourselves have set in motion. But the effect to ourselves will be precisely the same as if they were brought about by the volition of an adverse personality. Thus, our inner workings of mind and Spirit directly influence the probabilities of future outcomes.

Fears and self-defeating thought can immobilize us from optimum interaction and harmony with the world. As such, the fear of utter uncertainty regarding the future can make life bitter and discouraging. The knowledge that we are dealing with a power that is no respecter of persons, and in which is no variability, which is, in fact, an unalterable Law, at once delivers us from all these terrors. Accordingly, we can alter the course of our daily peace of mind and our destiny in general.

George Mentz, JD, MBA

The laws of nature do not harbor revenge. Once we adapt our methods to their character, they will work for us without taking any retrospective notice of our past errors. The law of Spirit may be more complex than that of electricity, because, as expressed in us, it is the law of conscious individuality, but it is nonetheless a purely natural law and follows the universal rule. Therefore we may dismiss from our minds, as a baseless figment, the fear of any divine power treasuring up anger against us, if we are sincerely seeking to do what is right in the here and now.

The new causes and impressions of universal thought energy that we put in motion now will produce their proper effect as surely as the old causes did; and thus by inaugurating a new sequence of good we shall cut off the old sequence of non-good. However, we cannot expect to bring about the new sequence while continuing to repeat the old causes, for the fruit must necessarily reproduce the nature of the seed.

Thus we are the masters of the situation, and, whether in this world or the next, it rests with ourselves either to perpetuate the self-defeating thought and character or to wipe it out and put in its place such things as excellence, good, kindness, beauty, thankfulness of mind, and love. And it may be noticed in passing that the great central Christian doctrine is based upon the most perfect knowledge of this law, and is the practical application to a profound problem of the deepest psychological science.

Much has been written and said on the origin of suffering or evil, and a volume might be filled with the detailed study of the subject. But for all practical purposes it may be summed up in one word: limitation. For what is the ultimate cause of all strife, whether public or private, but the notion that the supply of good is limited? With the bulk of mankind this is a fixed idea, and they therefore argue that because there is only a certain limited quantity of good or things, the share in their possession can be increased only by correspondingly diminishing someone else's share.

Anyone entertaining the same idea, naturally resents the attempt to deprive others of any portion of this "limited" quantity; and hence arises the whole crop of envy, hatred, fraud, and violence, whether between individuals, classes, or nations.

If people only realized the truth that good is not a certain limited quantity, but a stream continuously flowing from the exhaustless infinite supply, and ready to take any direction we choose to give it. Further, each one is able by the action of his or her own mind and thought to draw from it indefinitely. As such, the substitution of this new and true idea for the old and false one of limitation would at one stroke remove all strife and struggle from the world. Then, every man would find a helper instead of a competitor in every other, and the very laws of Nature would be found a ceaseless source of profit and delight. The man who has realized his true relation as a son to his father and who is in tune with the Infinite has harnessed and cultivated the greatest of all powers. And this principle of sonship raises man from the condition of bondage as a servant by reason of limitation to the status of a son by the entire removal of all limitations.

To believe and act on this principle is to believe on the Son of God, and a practical belief in our own sonship thus sets us free from all evil and from all fear of evil. It brings us out of the well of despondency into the kingdom of life. Like everything else, it has to grow, but the good seed of liberating Truth once planted in the heart is sure to germinate with a mighty power, and the more we endeavor to foster its growth, the more rapidly we shall find our lives increase in richness--a joy to ourselves, a brightness to our homes, and a blessing expanding to all around in ever-widening circles. Enough has now been said to show the identity of principle between the teaching of the great scripture and that of metaphysics. But the hints contained in the foregoing papers will, I hope, suffice to show that there is nothing antagonistic between the two systems, or, rather, to show that they are one--the statement of the One Truth, which always has been and always will be.

And if what I have now endeavored to put before my readers should lead any of them to follow up the subject more fully for themselves, I can promise them an inexhaustible store of wonder, delight, and strength in the study of these universal truths.

Dr. Charles F. Haanel, PhD, Psy. D. – The Principles of the Master Key System in 24 Parts – Circa 1912

Introduction: Nature compels us all to move through life. We could not remain stationary however much we wished. Every right-thinking person wants not merely to move through life like a sound-producing, perambulating plant, but to develop - to improve - and to continue the development mentally to the close of physical life.

Some men seem to attract success, power, wealth, attainment, with very little conscious effort; others conquer with great difficulty; still others fail altogether to reach their ambitions, desires and ideals. Why is this so? Why should some men realize their ambitions easily, others with difficulty, and still others not at all?

1. The attitude of mind necessarily depends upon what we think. Therefore, the secret of all power, all achievement and all possession depends upon our method of thinking. The world without is a reflection of the world within. Harmony in the world within means the ability to control our thoughts, and to determine for ourselves how any experience is to affect us.

2. Our difficulties are largely due to confused ideas and ignorance of our true interests. Thought is energy. Active thought is active energy; concentrated thought is a concentrated energy. Thought concentrated on a definite purpose becomes power. This is the power which is being used by those who do not believe in the virtue of poverty, or the beauty of self-denial. They perceive that this is the talk of weaklings.

The value of the subconscious is enormous; it inspires us; it warns us; it furnishes us with names, facts and scenes from the storehouse of memory. It directs our thoughts, tastes, and accomplishes tasks so intricate that no conscious mind, even if it had the power, has the capacity for. On the spiritual side, it is the source of ideals, of aspiration, of the imagination, and is the channel through which we recognize our Divine Source, and in proportion as we recognize this divinity do we come into an understanding of the source of power.

3. It is our attitude of mind toward life which determines the experiences with which we are to meet; if we expect nothing, we shall have nothing; if we demand much, we shall receive the greater portion. The world is harsh only as we fail to assert ourselves. The criticism of the world is bitter only to those who cannot compel room for their ideas. It is fear of this criticism that causes many ideas to fail to see the light of day.

Exercise: I want you to not only be perfectly still, and inhibit all thought as far as possible, but relax, let go, let the muscles take their normal condition; this will remove all pressure from the nerves, and eliminate that tension which so frequently produces physical exhaustion.

4. The greatest and most marvelous power which this "I" has been given is the power to think, but few people know how to think constructively, or correctly, consequently they achieve only indifferent results. Most people allow their thoughts to dwell on selfish purposes, the inevitable result of an infantile mind. When a mind becomes mature, it understands that the germ of defeat is in every selfish thought.

One of the strongest affirmations which you can use for the purpose of strengthening the will and realizing your power to accomplish, is, "I can be what I will to be." Every time you repeat it realize who and what this "I" is; try to come into a thorough understanding of the true nature of the "I"; if you do, you will become invincible; that is, provided that your objects and purposes are constructive and are therefore in harmony with the creative principle of the Universe.

5. In the domain of mind and spirit, in the domain of practical power, such an estate is yours. You are the heir! You can assert your heirship and possess, and use this rich inheritance. Power over circumstances is one of its fruits, and health, harmony and prosperity are assets upon its balance sheet. It offers you poise and peace. It costs you only the labor of studying and harvesting its great resources. It demands no sacrifice, except the loss of your limitations, your servitudes, your weakness. It clothes you with self-honor, and puts a scepter in your hands. To gain this estate, three processes are necessary: You must earnestly desire it. You must assert your claim. You must take possession.

Exercise: Now, go to your room, enter your relaxed state, and mentally select a place which has pleasant associations. Make a complete mental picture of it, see the buildings, the grounds, the trees, friends, associations, everything complete. At first, you will find yourself thinking of everything under the sun, except the ideal upon which you desire to concentrate. But do not let that discourage you. Persistence will win, but persistence requires that you practice these exercises every day without fail.

6. To be in tune with eternal truth we must possess poise and harmony within. In order to receive intelligence the receiver must be in tune with the transmitter. Every thought sets the brain cells in action; at first the substance upon which the thought is directed fails to respond, but if the thought is sufficiently refined and concentrated, the substance finally yields and expresses perfectly. Finding harmony with the universal power will bring you great power and resources.

7. Visualization is the process of making mental images, and the image is the mold or model which will serve as a pattern from which your future will emerge. Make the image clear and clean-cut, hold it firmly in the mind and you will gradually and constantly bring the thing nearer to you. You can be what "you will to be." You should see the end before a single step is taken; so you are to picture in your mind what you want; you are sowing the seed, but before sowing any seed you want to know what the harvest is to be.

This is Idealization. If you are not sure, return to the quiet meditation or prayer daily until the picture becomes plain. Make the Mental Image; make it clear, distinct, perfect; hold it firmly; the ways and means will develop; supply will follow the demand; you will be led to do the right thing at the right time and in the right way. Earnest Desire will bring about Confident Expectation, and this in turn must be reinforced by Firm Demand.

Exercise: Visualize a friend, see your friend exactly as you last saw him, see the room, the furniture, recall the conversation, now see his face, see it distinctly, now talk to him about some subject of mutual interest; see his expression change, watch him smile. Can you do this?

8. As the one purpose of life is growth, all principles underlying existence must contribute to give it effect. Thought, therefore, takes form and the law of growth eventually brings it into manifestation. You may freely choose what you think, but the result of your thought is governed by an immutable law. Any line of thought persisted in cannot fail to produce its result in the character, health and circumstances of the individual.

The law of attraction will certainly and unerringly bring to you the conditions, environment, and experiences in life, corresponding with your habitual, characteristic, predominant mental attitude. Not what you think once in a while when you are in church, or have just read in a good book, BUT your predominant mental attitude is what counts.

Combining harmonious thought and visualization with the great powers within is where true energy and creation comes from. Place yourself in position to receive this power. As it is Omnipresent, it must be within you. We know that this is so because we know that all power is from within, but it must be developed, unfolded, & cultivated; in order to do this we must be receptive and open.

9. Hold in mind the condition desired; affirm it as an already existing fact. This indicates the value of a powerful affirmation. By constant repetition it becomes a part of ourselves. We are actually changing ourselves; are making ourselves what we want to be.

To think correctly, accurately, we must know the "Truth." We must realize that truth is the vital principle of the Universal Mind and is Omnipresent. For instance, if you require health, a realization of the fact that the "I" in you is spiritual and that all spirit is one; that wherever a part is the whole must be, will bring about a condition of health, because every cell in the body must manifest the truth as you see it.

If you require Love try to realize that the only way to get love is by giving it, that the more you give the more you will get, and the only way in which you can give it, is to fill yourself with it, until you become a magnet.

If you require Wealth a realization of the fact that the "I" in you is one with the Universal mind which is all substance, and is Omnipotent, will assist you in bringing into operation the law of attraction which will bring you into vibration with those forces which make for success and bring about conditions of power and affluence in direct proportion with the character and purpose of your affirmation and thinking. The affirmation, "I am whole, perfect, strong, powerful, loving, harmonious and happy", will bring about harmonious conditions. The reason for this is because the affirmation is in strict accordance with the Truth, and when truth appears every form of error or discord must necessarily disappear. You have found that the "I" is spiritual, it must necessarily then always be no less than perfect, the affirmation. "I am whole, perfect, strong, powerful, loving, harmonious and happy" is therefore an exact scientific statement.

Whatever you desire for yourself, affirm it for others, and it will help you both. We reap what we sow. If we send out thoughts of love and health, they return to us like bread cast upon the waters…

10. Abundance is a natural law of the Universe. The evidence of this law is conclusive; we see it on every hand. Everywhere Nature is lavish, wasteful, and extravagant.

The man who understands that there is no effect without an adequate cause thinks impersonally. He gets down to bedrock facts regardless of consequences.

Thought is the connecting link between the Infinite and the finite, between the Universal and the individual. Constructive thought must necessarily be creative, but creative thought must be harmonious, and this eliminates all destructive or competitive thought.

Exercise: Select a blank space on the wall, or any other convenient spot, from where you usually sit, mentally draw a black horizontal line about six inches long, try to see the line as plainly as though it were painted on the wall; now mentally draw two vertical lines connecting with this horizontal line at either end; now draw another horizontal line connecting with the two vertical lines; now you have a square. Try to see the square perfectly; when you can do so draw a circle within the square; now place a point in the center of the circle; now draw the point toward you about 10 inches; now you have a cone on a square base; you will remember that your work was all in black; change it to white, to red, to yellow.

Many fail because, they do not understand the law; there is no link to universal mind; they have not formed the connection. The remedy is a conscious recognition of the law of attraction with the intention of bringing the best into existence for a definite purpose. If done rightly, thought will correlate with its object (what you want) and bring it into manifestation, because thought is a product of the spiritual man, and spirit is the creative Principle of the Universe.

11. While every effect is the result of a cause, the effect in turn becomes a cause, which creates other effects, which in turn create still other causes; so that when you put the law of attraction into operation you must remember that you are starting a train of causation for good or otherwise which may have endless possibilities. We are first to believe that our desire has already been fulfilled, its accomplishment will then follow. This is a concise direction for making use of the creative power of thought by impressing on the Universal subjective mind, the particular thing which we desire as an already existing fact.

This conception is also elaborated upon by Swedenborg in his doctrine of correspondences; and a still greater teacher has said, "What things soever ye desire, when ye pray, believe that ye receive them, and ye shall have them." (Mark 11:24) The difference of the tenses in this passage is remarkable. "Faith is the substance of things hoped for, the evidence of things unseen." The Law of Attraction is the Law by which Faith is brought into manifestation. This law has eliminated the elements of uncertainty and caprice from men's lives and substituted law, reason, and certitude.

Exercise: Concentrate on the quotation taken from the Bible, "Whatsoever things ye desire, when ye pray, believe that ye receive them and ye shall have them"; notice that there is no limitation, "Whatsoever things" is very definite and implies that the only limitation which is placed upon us in our ability to think, to be equal to the occasion, to rise to the emergency, to remember that Faith is not a shadow, but a substance, "the substance of things hoped for, the evidence of things not seen."

12. "You must first have the knowledge of your power; second, the courage to dare; third, the faith to do." It is the combination of Thought and Love which forms the irresistible force, called the law of attraction. All natural laws are irresistible, the law of Gravitation, or Electricity, or any other law operates with mathematical exactitude.

The intention governs the attention. Things are created in the mental or spiritual world before they appear in the outward act or event by the simple process of governing our thought forces today, we help create the events which will come into our lives in the future, perhaps even tomorrow.

Exercise: Get into the same relaxed state in the same position as you were previously; let go, both mentally and physically; always do this; never try to do any mental work under pressure; see that there are no tense muscles or nerves, that you are entirely comfortable. Now realize your unity with omnipotence; get into touch with this power, come into a deep and vital understanding, appreciation, and realization of the fact that your ability to think is your ability to act upon the Universal Mind, and bring it into manifestation, realize that it will meet any and every requirement; that you have exactly the same potential ability which any individual ever did have or ever will have, because each is but an expression or manifestation of the One, all are parts of the whole, there is no difference in kind or quality, the only difference being one of degree.

13. Part Thirteen which follows tells why the dreams of the dreamer come true. It explains the law of causation by which dreamers, inventors, authors, financiers, bring about the realization of their desires. It explains the law by which the thing pictured upon our mind eventually becomes our own. Every individual who ever advanced a new idea, whether a Columbus, a Darwin, a Galileo, a Fulton or an Emerson, was subjected to ridicule or persecution; so that this objection should receive no serious consideration; but, on the contrary, we should carefully consider every fact which is brought to our attention; by doing this we will more readily ascertain the law upon which it is based.

In creating a Mental Image or an Ideal, we are projecting a thought into the Universal Substance (The Whole) from which all things are created. This means that recognition of Universal Substance brings about realization and a connection. When this tremendous fact begins to permeate your consciousness, when you really come into a realization of the fact that you (not your body, but the Ego), the "I," the spirit which thinks is an integral part of the great whole, that it is the same in substance, in quality, in kind, that the Creator could create nothing different from Himself, you will also be able to say, "The Father and I are one" and you will come into an understanding of the beauty, the grandeur, & the transcendental opportunities which have been placed at your disposal.

Exercise: Make use of the principle, recognize the fact that you are a part of the whole, and that a part must be the same in kind and quality as the whole; the only difference there can possibly by, is in degree. If connected and in tune, then your thoughts are mind are in fact heard and received by Creation.

14. Thought is a spiritual activity and is therefore endowed with creative power. This does not mean that some thought is creative, but that all thought is creative. Mankind is part of all there is. Our mind is connected to our body and to Spirit. Each cell is born, reproduces itself, dies and is absorbed. The maintenance of health and life itself depends upon the constant regeneration of these cells.

This change or growth of thought or enhancement of your mental attitude will not only bring you the material things which are necessary for your highest and best welfare, but will bring health and harmonious conditions generally. Imagine over time that your body, organs, and cells being are being regenerated to perfection and the old cells being cast away. In the same way, your power to attract the best from the world may operate if you are harmonious in mind, constructive in word and deed, and into action.

Exercise: Concentrate on Harmony, and when I say concentrate, I mean all that the word implies; concentrate so deeply, so earnestly, that you will be conscious of nothing but harmony. Remember, we learn by doing. Reading these lessons will get you nowhere. It is in the practical application that the value consists.

15. Difficulties and obstacles, indicate that we are either refusing to let go of what we no longer need, or refusing to accept what we require. Haanel gives a scientific example of a tiny parasite that adapts and grows wings rather than dying. In this way, people always have the inclination to adapt, improve and innovate. The question is when and how? Unfortunately, many times we are taught the same harmful lesson over and over until we are forced to take risk and truly change. To truly change, we must alter mind and spirit with our thoughts. In order to possess vitality, thought must be impregnated with love. Love is a product of the emotions. Therefore, thought and constructive emotion such as: Love, Gratitude, Faith and even Hope will most certainly stimulate the forces of the universe to assist you in your journey. This leads to the inevitable conclusion that if we wish to express abundance in our lives, we can afford to think abundance only, and as words are only thoughts taking form, we must be especially careful to use nothing but constructive and harmonious language, which when finally crystallized into objective forms, will prove to our advantage. This wonderful power of clothing thoughts in the form of words is what differentiates man from the rest of the animal kingdom. Words are thoughts and are therefore an invisible and invincible power which will finally objectify themselves in the form they are given. Overall, we may use constructive thinking and speech to master our destiny. To overcome error thoughts, we may use a conscious realization of the fact that Truth invariably destroys error. We do not have to laboriously shovel the darkness out; all that is necessary is to turn on the light. The same principle applies to every form of negative thought.

Exercise: Concentrate on Insight; take your accustomed relaxed position and focus the thought on the fact that to have a knowledge of the creative power of thought does not mean to possess the art of thinking. Let the thought dwell on the fact that knowledge does not apply itself. Our actions are not governed by knowledge, but by custom, precedent and habit. i.e. (Mental and Physical). That the only way we can get ourselves to apply knowledge is by a determined conscious effort. Call to mind the fact that knowledge unused passes from the mind, that the value of the information is in the application of the principle; continue this line of thought until you gain sufficient insight to formulate a definite program for applying this principle to your own particular problem.

16. Wealth should then never be desired as an end, but simply as a means of accomplishing an end. Success is contingent upon a higher goal ideal than the mere accumulation of riches, and he who aspires to such success must formulate an ideal for which he is willing to strive. Therefore, the essence of what we will do with wealth must be codified into a purpose of mind and desire. Haanel poses this question to a multi-millionaire with a railroad empire.... "Did you actually vision to yourself the whole thing? I mean, did you, or could you, really close your eyes and see the tracks? And the trains running? And hear the whistles blowing? Did you go as far as that?" "Yes." "How clearly?" "Very clearly."

Visualization must, of course, be directed by the will; we are to visualize exactly what we want; we must be careful not to let the imagination run riot. Thought is the plastic material with which we build images of our growing conception of life. Use determines its existence. We can form our own mental images, through our own interior processes of thought regardless of the thoughts of others, regardless of exterior conditions, regardless of environment of every kind, and it is by the exercise of this power that we can control our own destiny, body, mind and soul. The result will depend upon the mental images from which it emanates; this will depend upon the depth of the impression, the predominance of the idea, the clarity of the vision, the boldness of the image.

Exercise: Try to bring yourself to a realization of the important fact that harmony and happiness are states of consciousness and do not depend upon the possession of things. Things are effects and come as a consequence of correct mental states. So that if we desire material possession of any kind our chief concern should be to acquire the mental attitude which will bring about the result desired. This mental attitude is brought about by a realization of our spiritual nature and our unity with the Universal Mind which is the substance of all things. This realization will bring about everything which is necessary for our complete enjoyment. This is scientific or correct thinking. When we succeed in bringing about this mental attitude it is comparatively easy to realize our desire as an already accomplished fact; when we can do this we shall have found the "Truth" which makes us "free" from every lack or limitation of any kind.

Haanel: "Scientific thinking is a recognition of the creative nature of spiritual energy and our ability to control it."

17. We are accustomed to look upon the Universe with a lens of five senses, and from these experiences our anthropomorphic conceptions originate, but true conceptions are only secured by spiritual insight. This insight requires a quickening of the vibrations of the Mind, and is only secured when the mind is continuously concentrated in a given direction. The subconscious mind may be aroused and brought into action in any direction and made to serve us for any purpose, by concentration. All mental discovery and attainment are the result of desire plus concentration; desire is the strongest mode of action; the more persistent the desire, the more authoritative the revelation. Desire added to concentration will wrench any secret from nature.

Vibration is the action of thought; it is vibration which reaches out and attracts the material necessary to construct and build. There is nothing mysterious concerning the power of thought; concentration simply implies that consciousness can be focalized to the point where it becomes identified with the object of its attention. Always concentrate on the ideal as an already existing fact; this is the life principle which goes forth and sets in motion those causes which guide, direct and bring about the necessary relation, which eventually manifest in form.

Exercise: Concentrate as nearly as possible in accordance with the method outlined in this lesson; let there be no conscious effort or activity associated with your purpose. Relax completely, avoid any thought of anxiety as to results. Remember that power comes through repose. Let the thought dwell upon your object, until it is completely identified with it, until you are conscious of nothing else. Lesson: If you wish to eliminate fear, concentrate on courage, if you wish to eliminate lack, concentrate on abundance, and if you wish to eliminate disease, concentrate on health.

Haanel: "Intuition usually comes in the Silence; great minds seek solitude frequently."

18. Thought is the invisible link by which the individual comes into communication with the Universal, the finite with the Infinite, the seen with the Unseen. Thought is the magic by which the human is transformed into a being who thinks and knows and feels and acts. Growth is conditioned on reciprocal action, and we find that on the mental plane like attracts like, that mental vibrations respond only to the extent of their vibratory harmony. It is clear, therefore, that thoughts of abundance and health will respond only to similar thoughts. The connecting link between the individual and the Universal is Thought, and Love and Inner Harmony (a powerful emotion and feeling) is what fuels thought into manifestation or cooperation from the universe.

Exercise: Concentrate upon your power to create; seek insight, perception; try to find a logical basis for the faith which is in you. Let the thought dwell on the fact that the physical man lives and moves and has his being in the sustainer of all organic life air, that he must breathe to live. Then let the thought rest on the fact that the spiritual man also lives and moves and has his being in a similar but subtler energy upon which he must depend for life, and that as in the physical world no life assumes form until after a seed is sown, and no higher fruit than that of the parent stock can be produced; so in the spiritual world no effect can be produced until the seed is sown and the fruit will depend upon the nature of the seed, so that the results which you secure depend upon your perception of law in the mighty domain of causation, the highest evolution of human consciousness.

19. In the Moral World we find the same law; we speak of good and evil, but Good is a reality, something tangible, while Evil is found to be simply a negative condition, the absence of Good. We know that the ability of the individual to think in constructive ways is his ability to act upon the Universal Mind and convert it into dynamic mind, or mind in motion. We have then come to know that Mind is the only principle which is operative in the physical, mental, moral and spiritual world.

Exercise: Concentrate, and when I use the word concentrate, I mean all that the word implies; become so absorbed in the object of your thought that you are conscious of nothing else, and do this a few minutes every day. You take the necessary time to eat in order that the body may be nourished, why not take the time to assimilate your mental food? Let the thought rest on the fact that appearances are deceptive. The earth is not flat, neither is it stationary; the sky is not a dome, the sun does not move, the stars are not small specks of light, and matter which was once supposed to be fixed has been found to be in a state of perpetual flux. Try to realize that the day is fast approaching -- its dawn is now at hand -- when modes of thought and action must be adjusted to rapidly increasing knowledge of the operation of eternal principles.

20. God is Spirit. Spirit is the Creative Principle of the Universe. Man is made in the image and likeness of God. Man is therefore a spiritual being. The only activity which spirit possesses is the power to think. Thinking is therefore a creative process. All form is therefore the result of the thinking process. When you begin to perceive that the essence of the Universal is within yourself -- is you -- you begin to do things; you begin to feel your power; it is the fuel which fires the imagination; which lights the torch of inspiration; which gives vitality to thought; which enables you to connect with all the invisible forces of the Universe. It is this power which will enable you to plan fearlessly, to execute masterfully. This "breath of life" is a superconscious reality. It is the essence of the "I am." It is pure "Being" or Universal Substance, and our conscious unity with it enables us to localize it, and thus exercise the powers of this creative energy. Thought which is in harmony with the Universal Mind will result in corresponding conditions. Thought which is destructive or discordant will produce corresponding results. You may use thought constructively or destructively, but the immutable law will not allow you to plant a thought of one kind and reap the fruit of another.

You may have all the wealth in the world, but unless you recognize it and make use of it, it will have no value; so with your spiritual wealth: unless you recognize it and use it, it will have no value.

Lesson: Inspiration is from within. The Silence is necessary, the senses must be stilled, the muscles relaxed, repose cultivated. When you have thus come into possession of a sense of poise and power you will be ready to receive the information or inspiration or wisdom which may be necessary for the development of your purpose.

Exercise: Go into the Silence and concentrate on the fact that "In him we live and move and have our being" is literally and scientifically exact! That you ARE because He IS, that if He is Omnipresent He must be in you. That if He is all in all you must be in Him! That He is Spirit and you are made in "His image and likeness" and that the only difference between His spirit and your spirit is one of degree, that a part must be the same in kind and quality as the whole. When you can realize this clearly you will have found the secret of the creative power of thought, you will have found the origin of both good and evil, you will have found the secret of the wonderful power of concentration, you will have found the key to the solution of every problem whether physical, financial, or environmental.

21. "A Master-Mind thinks big thoughts. The creative energies of mind find no more difficulty in handling large situations, than small ones." Everything which we hold in our consciousness for any length of time becomes impressed upon our subconscious and so becomes a pattern which the creative energy will wave into our life and environment. This is the secret of the wonderful power of prayer The real secret of power is consciousness of power. The Universal Mind is unconditional; therefore, the more conscious we become of our unity with this mind, the less conscious we shall become of conditions and limitations, and as we become emancipated or freed from conditions we come into a realization of the unconditional. We have become free! Thus, prayer, meditation, and focused thought can be extremely effective in reaching your heights.

It is no easy matter to change the mental attitude, but by persistent effort it may be accomplished. The mental attitude is patterned after the mental pictures which have been photographed on the brain. If you do not like the pictures, destroy the negatives and create new pictures; this is the art of visualization. The Divine Mind makes no exceptions to favor any individual; but when the individual understands and realizes his Unity with the Universal principle he will appear to be favored because he will have found the source of all health, all wealth, and all power.

Exercise: Concentrate on the Truth. Try to realize that the Truth shall make you free, that is, nothing can permanently stand in the way of your perfect success when you learn to apply the scientifically correct thought methods and principles. Realize that you are externalizing in your environment your inherent soul potencies. Realize that the Silence offers an ever-available and almost unlimited opportunity for awakening the highest conception of Truth. Try to comprehend that Omnipotence itself is absolute silence, all else is change, activity, limitation. Silent thought concentration is therefore the true method of reaching, awakening, and then expressing the wonderful potential power of the world within.

22. Thoughts are spiritual seeds, which, when planted in the subconscious mind, have a tendency to sprout and grow, but unfortunately the fruit is frequently not to our liking. To remain healthy and regain health, we must increase the inflow and distribution of vital energy throughout the system, and this can only be done by eliminating thoughts of fear, worry, care, anxiety, jealousy, hatred, and every other destructive thought, which tend to tear down and destroy optimal health. It is through the law of vibration that the mind exercises this control over the body. We know that every mental action is a vibration, and we know that all form is simply a mode of motion, a rate of vibration. Therefore, any given vibration immediately modifies every atom in the body, every life cell is affected and an entire chemical change is made in every group of life cells. Through cooperation with our body, cell life and regeneration can be maintained at its highest levels.

Exercise: Concentrate on Tennyson's beautiful lines "Speak to Him, thou, for He hears, and spirit with spirit can meet, Closer is He than breathing, and nearer than hands and feet." Then try to realize that when you do "Speak to Him" you are in touch with Omnipotence. This realization and recognition of this Omnipresent power will quickly destroy any and every form of sickness or suffering and substitute harmony and perfection. Of course we should see a doctor if they can remove an infection and fix a problem. Thus, we should cooperate with all those available who should help us in a truthful manner while also cooperating with our bodies and spirit to heal, regenerate, and reach abundance. You will then more readily appreciate the ideal man, the man made in the image and likeness of God, and you will more readily appreciate the all originating Mind that forms, upholds, sustains, originates, and creates all there is.

23. One of the highest laws of success is service. Service to yourself and to humanity. It is inevitable that the entertainment of positive, constructive and unselfish thoughts should have a far-reaching effect for good. Compensation is the keynote of the universe. Nature is constantly seeking to strike an equilibrium. Where something is sent out something must be received; else there should be a vacuum formed.

You can make a money magnet of yourself, but to do so you must first consider how you can make money for other people. We make money by making friends, and we enlarge our circle of friends by making money for them, by helping them, by being of service to them. The first law of success then is service, and this in turn is built on integrity and justice. Keep in mind, generous thoughts filled with strength and vitality. Giving without expectation will form a vacuum which must be filled. Therefore, the laws of cause and effect will favor you with your sincere assistance and service to others.

Helping Others Mentally: If you desire to help someone, to destroy some form of lack, limitation or error, the correct method is not to think of the person whom you wish to help; the intention to help them is entirely sufficient, as this puts you in mental touch with the person. Then drive out of your own mind any belief of lack, limitation, disease, danger, difficulty or whatever the trouble might be. As soon as you have succeeded is doing this the result will have been accomplished, and the person will be free.

Attention develops concentration, and concentration develops Spiritual Power, and Spiritual Power is the mightiest force in existence. The power of attention is called concentration; this power is directed by the will; for this reason we must refuse to concentrate or think of anything except the things we desire. "Spirituality" is quite "practical," very "practical," intensely "practical." It teaches that Spirit is the Real Thing, the Whole Thing, and that Matter is but plastic stuff, which Spirit is able to create, mould, manipulate, and fashion to its will. Spirituality is the most "practical" thing in the world -- the only really and absolutely "practical" thing that there is!

Exercise: Concentrate on the fact that man is not a body with a spirit, but a spirit with a body, and that it is for this reason that his desires are incapable of any permanent satisfaction in anything not spiritual. Money is therefore of no value except to bring about the conditions which we desire, and these conditions are necessarily harmonious. Harmonious conditions necessitate sufficient supply, so that if there appears to be any lack, we should realize that the idea or soul of money is service, and as this thought takes form, channels of supply will be opened, and you will have the satisfaction of knowing that spiritual methods are entirely practical.

24. If you have practiced each of the exercises a few minutes every day, as suggested, you will have found that you can get out of life exactly what you wish by first putting into life that which you wish. Every form of concentration, forming Mental Images, Constructive Argument, and Autosuggestion are all simply methods by which you are enabled to realize the Truth.

When you master these steps, you will have mastered TRUTH. The method for removing this error is to go into the Silence and know the Truth; as all mind is one mind, you can do this for yourself or anyone else. If you have learned to form mental images of the conditions desired, this will be the easiest and quickest way to secure results; if not, results can be accomplished by argument, by the process of convincing yourself absolutely of the truth of your statement.

The absolute truth is that the "I" is perfect and complete; the real "I" is spiritual and can therefore never be less than perfect; it can never have any lack, limitation, or disease. The flash of genius does not have origin in the molecular motion of the brain; it is inspired by the ego, the spiritual "I" which is one with the Universal Mind, and it is our ability to recognize this Unity which is the cause of all inspiration, all genius.

Most people understand this word "GOD" to mean something outside of themselves; while exactly the contrary is the fact. It is our very life. Without it we would be dead. We would cease to exist. The minute the spirit leaves the body, our bodies are as nothing. Therefore, spirit is really, all there is of us. When the truth of this statement is realized, understood, and appreciated, you will have come into possession of the Master-Key.

Now, the only activity which the spirit possesses is the power to think. Therefore, thought must be creative, because spirit is creative. This creative power is impersonal and your ability to think is your ability to control it and make use of it for the benefit of yourself and others. The conditions with which you meet in the world without are invariably the result of the conditions obtaining in the world within, therefore it follows with scientific accuracy that by holding the perfect ideal in mind you can bring about ideal conditions in your environment. What is meant by thinking? Clear, decisive, calm, deliberate, sustained thought with a definite end in view. What will be the result? You will also be able to say, "It is not I that doeth the works, but the 'Father' that dwelleth within me, He doeth the works." You will come to know that the "Father" is the Universal Mind and that He does really and truly dwell within you, in other words, you will come to know that the wonderful promises made in the Bible are fact, not fiction, and can be demonstrated by anyone having sufficient understanding.

Codified, Revised and Extracted from the Master Key System by Dr. Haanel. Revisions by Prof. Mentz.

Dr. William W. Atkinson - Secret of Success – 1907 - Also known as: Swami Panchadasi, & Magus Incognitus

Laws of Attraction

Desire is the motivating force that moves the Will into action, and which cause the varied activity of life, men and things. Desire-Force is a real power in life, and influences not only tracts, influences and compels other persons and things to swing in toward the center of the Desire sending forth the currents. In the Secret of Success, Desire plays a prominent part. Without a Desire for Success, there is no Success, none. The Law of Attraction is set into motion by Desire.

The mental process has aptly been spoken of as "vibrations," a figure that has a full warrant in modern science. Then, by raising the vibration to the Positive pitch, the negative vibrations may be counteracted while positive outcomes will increase.

Desire

We should Desire firmly, confident, and earnestly. Be not half-hearted in your demands and desires – claim and demand the WHOLE THING, and feel confident that it will work out into material objectivity and reality. Think of it, dream of it, and always LONG for it – you must learn to want it the worst way – learn to "want it hard enough. "You can attain and obtain many things by "wanting them hard enough" – the trouble is with most of us that we do not want things hard enough – we mistake vague cravings and wished for earnest, longing, demanding Desire and Want. Get to Desire and Demand the Thing just as you demand and Desire your daily meals. That is "wanting it the worst way. "This is merely a hint – surely you can supply the rest, if you are in earnest, and "want to hard enough. "

Personal Magnetism

People's mental states are "contagious," and if one infuses enough life and enthusiasm into his mental states they will affect the minds of persons with whom they come in contact. Enthusiasm gives Earnestness to the person, and there is no mental state so effective as Earnestness. Earnestness makes itself felt strongly, and will often make a person give you attention in spite of him self.

All of us emit a sphere, aura, or halo, impregnated with the very essence of ourselves; people know it; so do our dogs and other pets; so does a hungry lion or tiger; aye, even flies, snakes and the insects, as we know to our cost. Some of us are magnetic – others not. Some of us are warm, attractive, love inspiring and friendship making, while others are cold, intellectual, thoughtful, reasoning, but not magnetic. Let a learned man of the latter type address an audience and it will soon tire of his intellectual discourse, and will manifest symptoms of drowsiness. He talks at them, but not into them – he makes them think, not feel, which is most tiresome to the majority of persons, and few speakers succeed who attempt to merely make people think – they want to be made to feel. People will pay liberally to be made to feel or laugh, while they will begrudge a dime for instruction or talk that will make them think. Pitted against a learned man of the type mentioned above, let there be a half-educated, but very loving, ripe and mellow man, with but nine-tenths of the logic and erudition of the first man, yet such a man carries along his crowd with perfect ease, and everybody is wide-awake, treasuring up every good thing that falls from his lips.

Attractive Personality

One of the first things that should be cultivated by those wishing to develop their Attraction of Personality is a mental atmosphere of Cheerfulness. There is nothing so invigorating as presence of a cheerful person – nothing so dispiriting as one of those Human Wet Blankets that cast a chill over everyone and everything with whom they come in contact.

Some of the benefits of cultivating a constructive personality are: (1) that they may induce a more buoyant and positive state of mind in themselves; (2) that they may attract cheerful persons and things to them by the Law of Attraction; and (3) that they may present an attractive Personality to others, and thereby be welcome and congenial associates and participants in the walks of life.

Another valuable bit of Personality is that of Self Respect. If you have real Self Respect it will manifest itself in your outward demeanor and appearance. If you don't have it, you had better start in and cultivate the appearance of Self Respect, and then Remember that you are a man, or a woman, as the case may be, and not a poor, crawling worm on the dust of a human door mat. Face the world firmly and fearlessly, keeping your eyes well to the front. HOLD YOUR HEAD HIGH.

Latent Powers – Willpower and Desire

Atkinson implies that we can use our will to force ourselves to get into the habit of thinking differently. We can cultivate higher thinking in many forms such as: constructive thinking, enthusiasm, desire, gratitude and more. Given the great, earnest, burning ardent Desire as an animating force – the great incentive to take action, and we are able to get up this mental "second-wind" – yes, third, fourth, and fifth winds – tapping one plane of inward power after another, until we work mental miracles.

Enthusiasm

A person filled with Enthusiasm seems indeed to be inspired by some power or being higher than himself – he taps on to a source of power of which he is not ordinarily conscious. And the result is that he becomes as a great magnet radiating attractive force in all directions and influencing those within his field of influence. For Enthusiasm is contagious and when really experienced by the individual renders him a source of inductive power, and a center of mental influence. But the power with which he is filled does not come from an outside source – it comes from certain inner regions of his mind or soul – from his Inner Consciousness.

Conclusion

We earnestly urge upon you to cultivate this "I AM" consciousness – that you may realize the Power Within you. The real Individual concealed behind the mask of Personality is YOU - the Real Self - the "I" - that part of you which you are conscious when you say "I AM," which is your assertion of existence and latent power. Remember, the "I" of "you" exists independent of the body. It means the state of being "animated," meaning, "possessed of life and vigor" - so that the state is really that of being filled with Power and Life. And that Power and Life comes from the very center of one's being - the "I AM" region of our mind and consciousness.

With a realization of the "I" or Real Self, comes a sense of Power that will manifest through you and make you strong. The awakening to a realization of the "I", in its clearness and vividness, will cause you to feel a sense of Being and Power that you have never before known. And then there will come naturally to you the correlated consciousness which expresses itself in the statement, "I CAN and I WILL," one of the grandest affirmations of Power that man can make. This "I Can and I Will" consciousness is that expression of the Something Within, which we trust that you will realize and manifest. We feel that behind all the advice that we can give you, this one thing is the PRIME FACTOR in the Secret of Success.

You can always get a better "running start" when in action, which will give you an advantage over the best "standing start" imaginable. Get into action and motion. We have endeavored to call your attention to something of far greater importance than a mere code of rules and general advice. We have pointed out to you the glorious fact that within each of you there is a Something Within, which if once aroused would give you a greatly increased power and capacity. And so we have tried to tell you this story of the Something Within, from different viewpoints, so that you might catch the idea in several ways. We firmly believe that Success depends most materially upon a recognition and manifestation of this Something Within.

The Plentiful Power of the Great Teacher: Dr. Joseph Murphy, PhD, D.R.S, D.D., LL.D

1. God wants us to be happy, successful, healthy, and to have a rich, abundant, and full life.
2. Your subconscious mind has powers that can be influenced by your conscious mind. Consistently making constructive impressions on your subconscious mind will soon change your thinking, your energy, your effectiveness, and your vibration.
3. Rejoice and be exceedingly glad that the Universe has blessed you, your family, your ideas and actions.
4. If there is lack in our lives, we need only to think and do something about it to improve our lot in life. Real inner change and outer character may be needed.
5. Money is only a medium of exchange and a symbol much like sheep or cattle have been in the past.
6. He believed that money is not the root of all evil unless you worship money in and of itself, which we all know is a violation of the laws of abundance. Peace of mind, balance, harmony, right mind, right action, and right livelihood will invariably lead to richness of life, which includes an abundance of money.
7. Success and money should be used to constructively serve humanity. Thus, the intention and essence of wealth must be known and directed in a manner that is good for all.
8. He believed that wealth was a state of mind, and the consciousness of poverty is not useful for anyone and can paralyze the student. Therefore, a change in consciousness to wealth and prosperity can indeed open the doors for ideas, opportunity, and blessings from the Supreme.
9. He believed that we should commune with universal mind and know and claim mentally and verbally that Spirit can and will bless us into prosperity.
10. Murphy believes in the source or Divine Mind and is the origin of all wealth. Thus, if we realize and connect to that source, our life and path will be abundant.
11. Murphy believed that concentrated thought charged with heart-felt emotion or feelings would almost certainly manifest over time.
12. When man operates on a level of thought that is harmonious and constructive, the Spiritual powers within and without will respond to our mind and actions.

13.   Whatever the mind dwells upon will expand and multiply in your life. Whatever the mind praises, blesses, and is thankful for will most probably increase in our life.

14.   Love is the most powerful feeling or Spirit energy. However, praise, thankfulness, gratitude, and peace are also just as powerful when continuously directed toward an objective such as a relationship, job, or goal.

15.   He suggests releasing your petitions to the Universe. Think it, feel it, claim it, mentally have it, mentally project it on your subconscious picture screen, but then *release* it with a sense of detachment, faith, and confidence where you know that the highest good and outcome will unfold.

16.   Murphy was a strong advocate of blessing those whom we would otherwise be jealous of. Thus, if somebody is doing well or become successful, then, we should mentally and verbally praise them whether friend or foe. The crux of this strategy is to think constructively without offsetting your vibration with opposite thoughts of envy and character assassination of others.

17.   Murphy agreed with Troward in this way: A person who has seen the end has effectively willed the means (the seed) to the realization of the end. It is up to us to cultivate the seed from that juncture.

18.   Murphy thinks that those who use constructive affirmations and who *know* in their heart with emotion that the affirmation is true, are consciously communing with the divine Spirit of abundance along with changing their individual character and consciousness for the better.

19.   Overall, Murphy believes that man's subconscious or inner Spirit is the root of self-enhancing power and the vital connection to Spiritual abundance. He believes that this part of the being can be affected by certain constructive habits and dominant thoughts. He tries to convey that one should muster the mind energy to will dominant thoughts over self-defeating ones.

20.   He encourages affirming what the heart, mind, and subconscious mind is *willing to* accept and *then* grow the essence of acceptance in that manner to prevent contradiction of mind. Thus, as a newer student of the philosophy, he suggests using statements that you can accept with minimal doubt such as, "I am getting better and better, or my income or business sales are increasing every day.

21.   Moreover, Murphy is also an promoter of relaxing the body, mind, and Spirit before making petitions to the Universe and to your inner subconscious. After getting into quiet communion with your higher self, you should use affirmations and visualizations with specificity and send them into the world after contemplation.

22.   Murphy uses the teachings of Jesus to emphasize that we do not need to live in the illusion of lack and poverty. There is plenty for all, and the Universe *will* simply create more for everyone when we are operating in the Spiritual dimension.

23.   Engage the mind-set of opulence. Imagine the end result of your short-term or long-term desires. Feel that it is true and a reality *right now* and rejoice in *it. Claim it* as *yours* in *mind.*

24.   Reject what seems to be true that is based only on apparent reality. Try to see beyond what your mind of lack wants you to see. Try to see the good in all and *not* just the inconvenience of a present, past, or future event.

25.   Murphy does state that your outer world is directly correlated to your inner thinking. Thus, we should try to correct any error thought and improve the quality of our thinking and Spirit connection.

26.   We should use prayer or quiet reflection to cleanse our mind and Spirit of self-defeating thoughts and to quit using destructive thoughts or the past as an excuse not to succeed.

27.   As for relationships, Murphy espoused that students should pray for others, forgive others, and develop harmony for others inside and out. It seems that he believes that we will have great relationships when we are spiritually whole, happy and at peace. Moreover, Murphy leads us to believe that we will attract greater relationships of love and trust when we become better and happier persons (filled with self-love) through the Spirit of attraction.

28.   He suggests that we should not allow fear, doubt, and commentary from others or from our own mind to blemish our new and improved mental outlook and visualizations.

29.   As an exercise, stand in the mirror and affirm health, wealth, peace, and success with amazing results. Keep doing this and see how your mind perception increases and changes for the good.

30.   One of Murphy's best exercises is the use of mental allegory. Thus, students can visualize themselves being congratulated for achieving some wonderful result, objective, or dream.

James Allen – As a Man Thinketh - 1902

Mind is the Master-power that molds and makes,
And Man is Mind, and evermore he takes
The tool of Thought, and, shaping what he wills
Brings forth a thousand joys, a thousand ills:--
He thinks in secret, and it comes to pass:
Environment is but his looking-glass

This little volume (the result of meditation and experience is not intended as an exhaustive treatise on the much-written-upon subject of the power of thought. It is suggestive rather than explanatory, its object being to stimulate men and women to the discovery and perception of the truth that--

"They themselves are makers of themselves"

by virtue of the thoughts which they choose and encourage; that mind is the master-weaver, both of the inner garment of character and the outer garment of circumstance, and that, as they may have hitherto woven in ignorance and pain they may now weave in enlightenment and happiness.

James Allen

George Mentz, JD, MBA

Thought and Character

The aphorism, "As a man thinketh in his heart so is he," not only embraces the whole of a man's being, but is so comprehensive as to reach out to every condition and circumstance of his life. A man is literally what he thinks, his character being the complete sum of all his thoughts.

As the plant springs from, and could not be without, the seed, so every act of man springs from the hidden seeds of thought, and could not have appeared without them. This applies equally to those acts called "spontaneous" and "unpremeditated" as to those which are deliberately executed.

Act is the blossom of thought, and joy and suffering are its fruit; thus does a man garner in the sweet and bitter fruitage of his own husbandry.

Man is a growth by law, and not a creation by artifice, and cause and effect are as absolute and undeviating in the hidden realm of thought as in the world of visible and material things. A noble and God-like character is not a thing of favor or chance, but is the natural result of continued effort in right thinking, the effect of long-cherished association with God-like thoughts. An ignoble and bestial character, by the same process, is the result of the continued harboring of groveling thoughts.

Man is made or unmade by himself. In the armory of thought he forges the weapons by which he destroys himself. He also fashions the tools with which he builds for himself heavenly mansions of joy and strength and peace. By the right choice and true application of thought, man ascends to the divine perfection. By the abuse and wrong application of thought he descends below the level of the beast. Between these two extremes are all the grades of character, and man is their maker and master.

Of all the beautiful truths pertaining to the soul which have been restored and brought to light in this age, none is more gladdening or fruitful of divine promise and confidence than this--that man is the master of thought, the molder of character, and the maker and shaper of condition, environment, and destiny.

As a being of power, intelligence, and love, and the lord of his own thoughts, man holds the key to every situation, and contains within himself that transforming and regenerative agency by which he may make himself what he wills.

Man is always the master, even in his weakest and most abandoned state. But in his weakness and degradation he is a foolish master who misgoverns his "household." When he begins to reflect upon his condition and search diligently for the law upon which his being is established, he then becomes the wise master, directing his energies with intelligence and fashioning his thoughts to fruitful issues. Such is the conscious master, and man can only thus become by discovering within himself the laws of thought. This discovery is totally a matter of application, self-analysis and experience.

Only by much searching and mining are gold and diamonds obtained, and man can find every truth connected with his being, if he will dig deep into the mine of his soul. That he is the maker of his character, the molder of his life, and the builder of his destiny, he may unerringly prove, if he will watch, control, and alter his thoughts, tracing their effects upon himself, upon others and upon his life and circumstances, linking cause and effect by patient practice and investigation. And utilizing his every experience, even the most trivial, everyday occurrence, as a means of obtaining that knowledge of himself which is understanding, wisdom, & power. In this direction is the law of absolute that "He that seeketh findeth; and to him that knocketh it shall be opened." For only by patience, practice, and ceaseless importunity can a man enter the door of the temple of knowledge.

Effect of Thought on Circumstances

A man's mind may be likened to a garden, which may be intelligently cultivated or allowed to run wild; but whether cultivated or neglected, it must, and will bring forth. If no useful seeds are put into it, then an abundance of useless weed-seeds will fall therein, and will continue to produce their kind.

Just as a gardener cultivates his plot, keeping it free from weeds, and growing the flowers and fruits which he requires so may a man tend the garden of his mind, weeding out all the wrong, useless and impure thoughts, and cultivating toward perfection the flowers and fruits of right, useful and pure thoughts. By pursuing this process, a man sooner or later discovers that he is the master-gardener of his soul, the director of his life. He also reveals, within himself, the flaws of thought, and understands, with ever-increasing accuracy, how the thought-forces and mind elements operate in the shaping of character, circumstances, and destiny.

Thought and character are one, and as character can only manifest and discover itself through environment and circumstance, the outer conditions of a person's life will always be found to be harmoniously related to his inner state. This does not mean that a man's circumstances at any given time are an indication of his entire character, but that those circumstances are so intimately connected with some vital thought-element within himself that, for the time being, they are indispensable to his development.

Every man is where he is by the law of his being; the thoughts which he has built into his character have brought him there, and in the arrangement of his life there is no element of chance, but all is the result of a law which cannot err. This is just as true of those who feel "out of harmony" with their surroundings as of those who are contented with them.

As a progressive and evolving being, man is where he is that he may learn that he may grow; and as he learns the spiritual lesson which any circumstance contains for him, it passes away and gives place to other circumstances.

Man is buffeted by circumstances so long as he believes himself to be the creature of outside conditions, but when he realizes that he is a creative power, and that he may command the hidden soil and seeds of his being out of which circumstances grow; he then becomes the rightful master of himself.

That circumstances grow out of thought every man knows who has for any length of time practiced self-control and self-purification, for he will have noticed that the alteration in his circumstances has been in exact ratio with his altered mental condition. So true is this that when a man earnestly applies himself to remedy the defects in his character, and makes swift and marked progress, he passes rapidly through a succession of vicissitudes.

The soul attracts that which it secretly harbors; that which it loves, and also that which it fears; it reaches the height of its cherished aspirations; it falls to the level of its unchastened desires and circumstances are the means by which the soul receives it own. Every thought-seed sown or allowed to fall into the mind, and to take root there, produces its own, blossoming sooner or later into act, and bearing its own fruitage of opportunity and circumstance. Good thoughts bear good fruit, bad thoughts bad fruit.

The outer world of circumstances shapes itself to the inner world of thought, and both pleasant and unpleasant external conditions are factors which make for the ultimate good of the individual. As the reaper of his own harvest, man learns both of suffering and bliss.

Following the inmost desires, aspirations, thoughts, by which he allows himself to be dominated (pursuing the will-o'-the wisps of impure imaginings or steadfastly walking the highway of strong and high endeavor), a man at last arrives at their fruition and fulfillment in the outer conditions of his life. The laws of growth and adjustment everywhere obtain.

A man does not come to the alms-house or the jail by the tyranny of fate or circumstance, but by the pathway of groveling thoughts and base desires. Nor does a pure-minded man fall suddenly into crime by stress of any mere external force; the criminal thought had long been secretly fostered in the heart, and the hour of opportunity revealed its gathered power. Circumstance does not make the man; it reveals him to himself.

No such conditions can exist as descending into vice and its attendant sufferings apart from vicious inclinations, or ascending into virtue and its pure happiness without the continued cultivation of virtuous aspirations; and man, therefore, as the lord and master of thought, is the maker of himself and the shaper of and author of environment. Even at birth the soul comes of its own and through every step of its earthly pilgrimage it attracts those combinations of conditions which reveal itself, which are the reflections of its own purity and impurity, its strength and weakness.

Men do not attract that which they want, but that which they are. Their whims, fancies, and ambitions are thwarted at every step, but their inmost thoughts and desires are fed with their own food, be it foul or clean. Man is manacled only by himself; thought and action are the jailors of Fate--they imprison, being base; they are also the angels of Freedom--they liberate, being noble. Not what he wished and prays for does a man get, but what he justly earns. His wishes and prayers are only gratified and answered when they harmonize with his thoughts and actions.

In the light of this truth what, then, is the meaning of "fighting against circumstances"? It means that a man is continually revolting against an effect without, while all the time he is nourishing and preserving its cause in his heart. That cause may take the form of a conscious vice or an unconscious weakness; but whatever it is, it stubbornly retards the efforts of it possessor, and thus calls aloud for remedy. Men are anxious to improve their circumstances, but are unwilling to improve themselves; they therefore remain bound. The man who does not shrink from self-crucifixion can never fail to accomplish the object upon which his heart is set. This is as true of earthly as of heavenly things. Even the man whose sole object is to acquire wealth must be prepared to make great personal sacrifices before he can accomplish his object; and how much more so he who would realize a strong and well-poised life?

It is pleasing to human vanity to believe that one suffers because of one's virtue; but not until a man has extirpated every sickly, bitter, and impure thought from his soul, can he be in a position to know and declare that his sufferings are the result of his good, and not of his bad qualities; and on the way to, yet long before he has reached that supreme perfection , he will have found, working in his mind and life, the great law which is absolutely just, and which cannot, therefore, give good for evil, evil for good. Possessed of such knowledge, he will then know, looking back upon his past ignorance and blindness, that his life is, and always was, justly ordered, and that all his past experiences, good and bad, were the equitable outworking of his evolving, yet unevolved self. Good thoughts and actions can never produce bad results; bad thoughts and actions can never produce good results. This is but saying that nothing can come from corn but corn, nothing from nettles but nettles. Men understand this law in the natural world, and work with it; but few understand it in the mental and moral world (though its operation there is just as simple and undeviating), and they, therefore, do not cooperate with it.

Suffering is always the effect of wrong thought in some direction. It is an indication that the individual is out of harmony with himself, with the law of his being. The sole and supreme use of suffering is to purify, to burn out all that is useless and impure. Suffering ceases for him who is pure. There could be no object in burning gold after the dross had been removed, and a perfectly pure and enlightened being could not suffer.

The circumstances which a man encounters with suffering are the result of his own mental disharmony. The circumstances which a man encounters with blessedness are the result of his own mental harmony. Blessedness, not material possessions, is the measure of right thought; wretchedness, not lack of material possessions, is the measure of wrong thought. A man may be cursed and rich; he may be blessed and poor. Blessedness and riches are only joined together when the riches are rightly and wisely used. And the poor man only descends into wretchedness when he regards his lot as a burden unjustly imposed.

Indigence and indulgence are the two extremes of wretchedness. They are both equally unnatural and the result of mental disorder. A man is not rightly conditioned until he is a happy, healthy, and prosperous being; and happiness, health, and prosperity are the result of a harmonious adjustment of the inner with the outer of the man with his surroundings.

A man only begins to be a man when he ceases to whine and revile, and commences to search for the hidden justice which regulates his life. And he adapts his mind to that regulating factor, he ceases to accuse others as the cause of his condition, and builds himself up in strong and noble thoughts; ceases to kick against circumstances, but beings to use them as aids to his more rapid progress, and as a means of discovering the hidden powers and possibilities within himself.

Law, not confusion, is the dominating principle in the universe; justice, not injustice, is the soul and substance of life. Righteousness, not corruption, is the molding and moving force in the spiritual government of the world.

This being so, man has but to right himself to find that the universe is right. And during the process of putting himself right, he will find that as he alters his thoughts towards things and other people, things and other people will alter towards him.

The proof of this truth is in every person, and it therefore admits of easy investigation by systematic introspection and self-analysis. Let a man radically alter his thoughts, and he will be astonished at the rapid transformation it will effect in the material conditions of his life. Men imagine that thought can be kept secret, but it cannot. It rapidly crystallizes into habit, and habit solidifies into circumstance. Bestial thoughts crystallize into habits of drunkenness and sensuality, which solidify into circumstances of destitution and disease. Impure thoughts of every kind crystallize into enervating and confusing habits, which solidify into distracting and adverse circumstances. Thoughts of fear, doubt, and indecision crystallize into weak, unmanly, and irresolute habits, which solidify into circumstances of failure, indigence, and slavish dependence. Lazy thoughts crystallize into weak, habits of uncleanliness and dishonesty, which solidify into circumstances of foulness and beggary. Hateful and condemnatory thoughts crystallize into habits of accusation and violence, which solidify into circumstances of injury and persecution. Selfish thoughts of all kinds crystallize into habits of self-seeking, which solidify into distressful circumstances.

On the other hand, beautiful thoughts of all kinds crystallize into habits of grace and kindliness, which solidify into genial and sunny circumstances. Pure thoughts crystallize into habits of temperance and self-control, which solidify into circumstances of repose and peace. Thoughts of courage, self-reliance, and decision crystallize into manly habits, which solidify into circumstances of success, plenty, and freedom. Energetic thoughts crystallize into habits of cleanliness and industry, which solidify into circumstances of pleasantness. Gentle and forgiving thoughts crystallize into habits of gentleness, which solidify into protective and preservative circumstances. Loving and unselfish thoughts which solidify into circumstances of sure and abiding prosperity and true riches.

A particular train of thought persisted in, be it good or bad, cannot fail to produce its results on the character and circumstances. A man cannot directly choose his circumstances, but he can choose his thoughts, and so indirectly, yet surely, shape his circumstances. Nature helps every man to gratification of the thoughts which he most encourages, and opportunities are presented which will most speedily bring to the surface both the good and the evil thoughts.

Let a man cease from his sinful thoughts, and all the world will soften towards him, and be ready to help him. Let him put away his weakly and sickly thoughts, and the opportunities will spring up on every hand to aid his strong resolves. Let him encourage good thoughts, and no hard fate shall bind him down to wretchedness and shame. The world is your kaleidoscope, and the varying combinations of colors which at every succeeding moment it presents to you are the exquisitely adjusted pictures of your ever-moving thoughts.

Effects of Thought on Body and Health

The body is the servant of the mind. It obeys the operations of the mind, whether they be deliberately chosen or automatically expressed. At the bidding of unlawful thoughts the body sinks rapidly into disease and decay; at the command of glad and beautiful thoughts it becomes clothed with youthfulness and beauty.

Disease and health, like circumstances, are rooted in thought. Sickly thoughts will express themselves through a sickly body. Thoughts of fear have been known to kill a man as speedily as a bullet and they are continually killing thousands of people just as surely though less rapidly. The people who live in fear of disease are the people who get it. Anxiety quickly demoralizes the whole body, and lays it open to the entrance of disease; while impure thoughts, even if not physically indulged, will sooner shatter the nervous system.

Strong pure, and happy thoughts build up the body in vigor and grace. The body is a delicate and plastic instrument, which responds readily to the thoughts by which it is impressed, and habits of thought will produce their own effects, good or bad, upon it.

Men will continue to have impure and poisoned blood, so long as they propagate unclean thoughts. Out of a clean heart comes a clean life and a clean body. Out of a defiled mind proceeds a defiled life and a corrupt body. Thought is the fount of action, life and manifestation; make the fountain pure, and all will be pure.

If you would perfect your body, guard your mind. If you would renew your body, beautify your mind. Thoughts of malice, envy, and disappointment, despondency, rob the body of its health and grace. A sour face does not come by chance; it is made by sour thoughts. Wrinkles that mar are drawn by folly, passion, pride. I know a woman of ninety-six who has the bright, innocent face of a girl. I know a man well under middle age whose face is drawn into in harmonious contours. The one is the result of a sweet and sunny disposition; the other is the outcome of passion and discontent.

As you cannot have a sweet and wholesome abode unless you admit the air and sunshine freely into your rooms, so a strong body and a bright, happy, or serene countenance can only result from the free admittance into the mind of thoughts of joy and goodwill and serenity. On the faces of the aged there are wrinkles made by sympathy others by strong and pure thought, and others are carved by passion; who cannot distinguish them? With those who have lived righteously, age is calm, peaceful, and softly mellowed, like the setting sun. I have recently seen a philosopher on his deathbed. He was not old except in years. He died as sweetly and peacefully as he had lived.

There is no physician like cheerful thought for dissipating the ills of the body; there is no comforter to compare with goodwill for dispersing the shadows of grief and sorrow. To live continually in thoughts of ill will, cynicism, suspicion, and envy, is to be confined in a self-made prison hole. But to think well of all, to be cheerful with all, to patiently learn to find the good in all--such unselfish thoughts are the very portals of heaven; and to dwell day by day in thoughts of peace toward every creature will bring abounding peace to their possessor

Thought and Purpose

Until thought is linked with purpose there is no intelligent accomplishment. With the majority the bark of thought is allowed to "drift" upon the ocean of life. Aimlessness is a vice, and such drifting must not continue for him who would street clear of catastrophe and destruction.

They who have no central purpose in their life fall an easy prey to petty worries, fears, troubles, and self-pitying, all of which are indications of weakness, which lead, just as surely as deliberately planned sins (though by a diff route), to failure, unhappiness, and loss, for weakness cannot persist in a power-evolving universe.

A man should conceive of a legitimate purpose in his heart, and set out to accomplish it. He should make this purpose the centralizing point of his thoughts. It may take the form of a spiritual ideal, or it may be a worldly object, according to his nature at the time being. Whichever it is, he should steadily focus his thought-forces upon the object he had set before him. He should make this purpose his supreme duty and should devote himself to its attainment, not allowing his thoughts to wander away into ephemeral fancies, longings, and imaginings. This is the royal road to self-control and true concentration of thought. Even if he fails again and again to accomplish his purpose--as he must until weakness is overcome--the strength of character gained will be the measure of his true success, and this will form a new starting point for future power and triumph.

Those who are not prepared for the apprehension of a great purpose, should fix the thoughts upon the faultless performance of their duty, no matter how insignificant their task may appear. Only in this way can the thoughts be gathered and focused, and resolution and energy be developed. Once this is done, there is nothing which may not be accomplished.

George Mentz, JD, MBA

The weakest soul knowing its own weakness, and believing
this truth--that strength can only be developed by effort and
practice--will, thus believing, at once begin to exert itself.
And, adding effort to effort, patience to patience, and
strength to strength, will never cease to develop and will at
last grow divinely strong. As the physically weak man can
make himself strong by careful and patient training, so the
man of weak thoughts can make them strong by exercising
himself in right thinking. To put away aimlessness and
weakness and to begin to think with purpose is to enter the
ranks of those strong ones who only recognize failure as
one of the pathways to attainment. Who make all conditions
serve them, and who think strongly, attempt fearlessly, and
accomplish masterfully.

Having conceived of his purpose, a man should mentally
mark out a straight pathway to its achievement, looking
neither to the right nor left. Doubts and fears should be
rigorously excluded. They are disintegrating elements
which break up the straight line of effort, rendering it
crooked, ineffectual, useless. Thoughts of doubt and fear
can never accomplish anything. They always lead to failure.
Purpose, energy, power to do, and all strong thoughts
cease when doubt and fear creep in.

The will to do springs from the knowledge that we can do.
Doubt and fear are the great enemies of knowledge, and he
who encourages them, who does not slay them, thwarts
himself at every step. He who has conquered doubt and
fear has conquered failure. His every thought is allied with
power, and all difficulties are bravely met and overcome.
His purposes are seasonably planted, and they bloom and
bring forth fruit that does not fall prematurely to the ground.

Thought allied fearlessly to purpose becomes creative
force. He who knows this is ready to become something
higher and stronger than a bundle of wavering thoughts and
fluctuating sensations. He who does this has become the
conscious and intelligent wielder of his mental powers.

Thoughts and Achievement

All that a man achieves and all that he fails to achieve is the direct result of his own thoughts. In a justly ordered universe, where loss of equipoise would mean total destruction, individual responsibility must be absolute. A man's weakness and strength, purity and impurity, are his own and not another man's. They are brought about by himself and not by another; and they can only be altered by himself, never by another. His condition is also his own, and not another man's. His sufferings and his happiness are evolved from within. As he thinks, so is he; as he continues to think, so he remains.

A strong man cannot help a weaker unless that weaker is willing to be helped. And even then the weak man must become strong of himself. He must, by his own efforts, develop the strength which he admires in another. None but himself can alter his condition.

It has been usual for men to think and to say, "Many men are slaves because one is an oppressor; let us hate the oppressor!" But there is amongst an increasing few a tendency to reverse this judgment and to say, "One man is an oppressor because many are slaves; let us despise the slaves."

The truth is that oppressor and slaves are cooperators in ignorance, and, while seeming to afflict each other, are in reality, afflicting themselves. A perfect knowledge perceives the action of law in the weakness of the oppressed and the misapplied power of the oppressor. A perfect love, seeing the suffering which both states entail, condemns neither; a perfect compassion embraces both oppressor and oppressed. He who has conquered weakness and has pushed away all selfish thoughts belongs neither to oppressor nor oppressed. He is free.

A man can only rise, conquer, and achieve by lifting up his thoughts. He can only remain weak, abject, and miserably by refusing to lift up his thoughts.

Before a man can achieve anything, even in worldly things, he must lift his thoughts above slavish animal indulgence. He may not, in order to succeed, give up all animal instincts and selfishness, necessarily, but a portion of it must, at least, be sacrificed. A man whose first thought is bestial indulgence could neither think clearly nor plan methodically. He could not find and develop his latent resources and would fail in any undertaking. Not having begun to manfully control his thoughts, he is not in a position to control affairs and to adopt serious responsibilities. He is not fit to act independently and stand alone. But he is limited only by the thoughts that he chooses.

There can be no progress nor achievement without sacrifice, and a man's worldly success will be by the measure that he sacrifices his confused animal thoughts, and fixes his mind on the development of his plans, and the strengthening of his resolution and self-reliance. The higher his he lifts his thoughts, the greater will be his success, the more blessed and enduring will be his achievements.

The universe does not favor the greedy, the dishonest, the vicious... although on the mere surface it sometimes may appear to do so. It helps the honest, the magnanimous, the virtuous. All the great teachers of the ages have declared this in varying ways, and to prove it and to know it a man has but to persist in making himself increasingly virtuous by lifting his thoughts.

Intellectual achievements are the result of thought consecrated to the search for knowledge or for the beautiful and true in nature. Such achievements may sometimes be connected with vanity and ambition, but they are not the outcome of those characteristics. They are the natural outgrowth of long and arduous effort, and of pure and unselfish thoughts.

Spiritual achievements are the consummation of holy aspirations. He who lives constantly in the conception of noble and lofty thoughts, who dwells upon all that is pure and selfless, will, as surely as the sun reaches its zenith and the moon its full, become wise and noble in character and rise into a position of influence and blessedness.

Achievement of any kind is the crown of effort, the diadem of thought. By the aid of self-control, resolution, purity, righteousness, and well-directed thought a man ascends. By the aid of animal instinct, indolence, impurity, corruption, and confusion of thought a man descends.

A man may rise to high success in the world, even to lofty attitudes in the spiritual realm, and again descend into weakness and wretchedness by allowing arrogant, selfish, and corrupt thoughts to take possession of him.

Victories attained by right thought can be maintained only by watchfulness. Many give way when success is assured, and rapidly fall back into failure.

All achievements, whether in the business, intellectual, or spiritual world, are the result of definitely directed thought, are governed by the same law, and are of the same method. The only difference is in the object of attainment.

He who would accomplish little need sacrifice little; he would would achieve much must sacrifice much. He who would attain highly must sacrifice greatly.

Vision and Ideals

The dreamers are the saviors of the world. As the visible world is sustained by the invisible, so men, through all their trials and sins and sordid vocations, are nourished by the beautiful visions of their solitary dreamers. Humanity cannot forget its dreamers; it cannot let their ideals fade and die; it lives in them; it knows them as the realities which it shall one day see and know.

Composer, sculptor, painter, poet, prophet, sage--these are the makers of the after-world, the architects of heaven. The world is beautiful because they have lived. Without them, laboring humanity would perish.

He who cherishes a beautiful vision, a lofty ideal in his heart, will one day realize it. Columbus cherished a vision of another world and he discovered it. Copernicus fostered the vision of a multiplicity of worlds and a wider universe, and he revealed it. Buddha beheld the vision of a spiritual world of stainless beauty and perfect peace, and he entered into it.

Cherish your visions; cherish your ideals. Cherish the music that stirs in your heart, the beauty that forms in your mind, the loveliness that drapes your purest thoughts. For out of them will grow all delightful conditions, all heavenly environment; of these, if you but remain true to them, your world will at last be built.

To desire is to obtain; to aspire is to achieve. Shall man's basest desires receive the fullest measure of gratification, and his purest aspirations starve for lack of sustenance? Such is not the Law. Such a condition can never obtain: "Ask and receive."

Dream lofty dreams, and as you dream, so shall you become. Your vision is the promise of what you shall one day be; your ideal is the prophecy of what you shall at last unveil.

The greatest achievement was at first and for a time a dream. The oak sleeps in the acorn; the bird waits in the egg. And in the highest vision of a soul a waking angle stirs. Dreams are the seedlings of realities.

Your circumstances may be uncongenial, but they shall not remain so if you only perceive an ideal and strive to reach it. You can't travel within and stand still without. Here is a youth hard pressed by poverty and labor. Confined long hours in an unhealthy workshop; unschooled and lacking all the arts of refinement. But he dreams of better things. He thinks of intelligence, or refinement, of grace and beauty. He conceives of, mentally builds up, an ideal condition of life. The wider liberty and a larger scope takes possession of him; unrest urges him to action, and he uses all his spare times and means to the development of his latent powers and resources. Very soon so altered has his mind become that the workshop can no longer hold him. It has become so out of harmony with his mind-set that it falls out of his life as a garment is cast aside. And with the growth of opportunities that fit the scope of his expanding powers, he passes out of it altogether. Years later we see this youth as a grown man. We find him a master of certain forces of the mind that he wields with worldwide influence and almost unequaled power. In his hands he holds the cords of gigantic responsibilities; he speaks and lives are changed; men and women hang upon his words and remold their characters. Sun-like, he becomes the fixed and luminous center around which innumerable destinies revolve. He has become the vision of his youth. He has become one with his ideal.

And you too, youthful reader, will realize the vision (not just the idle wish) of your heart, be it base or beautiful, or a mixture of both. For you will always gravitate toward that which you, secretly, most love. Into your hands will be placed the exact results of your own thoughts. You will receive that which you earn; no more, no less. Whatever your present environment may be, you will fall, remain, or rise with your thoughts--your vision, your ideal. You will become as small as your controlling desire; as great as your dominant aspiration.

The thoughtless, the ignorant, and the indolent, seeing only the apparent effects of things and not the things themselves, talk of luck, of fortune, and chance. Seeing a man grow rich, they say, "How lucky he is!" Observing another become skilled intellectually, they exclaim, "How highly favored he is!" And noting the saintly character and wide influence of another, they remark, "How chance helps him at every turn!" They do not see the trials and failures and struggles which these men have encountered in order to gain their experience. They have no knowledge of the sacrifices they have made, of the undaunted efforts they have put forth, of the faith they have exercised so that they might overcome the apparently insurmountable and realize the vision of their heart.

They do not know the darkness and the heartaches; they only see the light and joy, and call it "luck." Do not see the long, arduous journey, but only behold the pleasant goal and call it "good fortune." Do not understand the process, but only perceive the result, and call it "chance." In all human affairs there are efforts, and there are results. The strength of the effort is the measure of the result. Change is not. Gifts, powers, material, intellectual and spiritual possessions are the fruits of effort. They are thoughts completed, objectives accomplished, visions realized.

The vision that you glorify in your mind, the ideal that you enthrone in your heart--this you will build your life by; this you will become.

Serenity and Peace of Mind

Calmness of mind is one of the beautiful jewels of wisdom. It is the result of long and patient effort in self-control. Its presence is an indication of ripened experience, and of a more than ordinary knowledge of the laws and operations of thought.

A man becomes calm in the measure that he understands himself as a thought-evolved being. For such knowledge necessitates the understanding of others as the result of thought, and as he develops a right understanding, and sees ever more clearly the internal relations of things by the action of cause and effect, he ceases to fuss, fume, worry, and grieve. He remains poised, steadfast, serene.

The calm man, having learned how to govern himself, knows how to adapt himself to others. And they, in turn reverence his spiritual strength. They feel that they can learn from him and rely upon him. The more tranquil a man becomes, the greater is his success, his influence, his power for good. Even the ordinary trader will find his business prosperity increase as he develops a greater self-control and equanimity, for people will always prefer to deal with a man whose demeanor is equitable.

The strong, calm man is always loved and revered. He is like a shade-giving tree in a thirsty land, or a sheltering rock in a storm. Who does not love a tranquil heart? a sweet-tempered, balanced life? It does not matter whether it rains or shines, or what changes come to those who possess these blessings for they are always serene and calm. That exquisite poise of character that we call serenity is the last lesson of culture. It is the flowering of life, the fruitage of the soul.

It is precious as wisdom--more desirable than fine gold. How insignificant mere money-seeking looks in comparison with a serene life. A life that dwells in the ocean of truth, beneath the waves, beyond the reach of the tempests, in the eternal calm!

How many people we know who sour their lives, who ruin all that is sweet and beautiful by explosive tempers, who destroy their poise of character and make bad blood! It is a question whether the great majority of people do not ruin their lives and mar their happiness by lack of self-control. How few people we meet in life who are well balanced, who have that exquisite poise which is characteristic of the finished character."

Yes, humanity surges with uncontrolled passion, is tumultuous with ungoverned grief, is blown about by anxiety and doubt. Only the wise man, only he whose thoughts are controlled and purified, makes the winds and the storms of the soul obey him.

Tempest-tossed souls, wherever you may be, under whatever conditions you may live, know this: In the ocean of life the isles of blessedness are smiling and the sunny shore of your ideal awaits your coming. Keep your hands firmly upon the helm of thought. In the core of your soul reclines the commanding Master; He does but sleep; wake Him. Self-control is strength. Right thought is mastery. Calmness is power. Say unto your heart, "Peace. Be still."

* From the works of James Allen – As a Man Thinketh 1902 *
Revised or Edited by Mentz

Eight Pillars of Prosperity: 1911 – Summary Concepts of James Allen's Forgotten Book of Secrets.

In James Allen's Eight Pillars of Prosperity, he teaches us of several keys to success and happiness. Allen believes that prosperity rests upon a moral and quasi spiritual foundation. The foundation consists of the Eight Pillars of which he explains include Energy, Economy, Integrity, System, Sympathy, Sincerity, Impartiality and Self-Reliance.

Energy

Energy should be directed and focused upon what you want to expand in your life. Negative focus can lead to a debilitating daily existence of frustration. Therefore, the concentration of your thoughts upon the best and being your best (in mind and action) can lead to a life of harmonious and effective living. Life will become easier as you are not resisting everything, but flowing with it & making an effective use of your decisions and energy. Don't worry about what was. Focus on what you want to become and how you can help others. Each day, engage in constructive tasks toward your dreams and building high character.

Other key terms to this step are: Promptness, Vigilance, and Industriousness, and Earnestness.

Economy

Economy has been addressed by the greats such as Ben Franklin and also in the ancient scriptures. There is no need to waste your time, energy or money. Making the best of your efforts and constructively use your assets and talents. There is no need for haste or waste. You can be creative and win without hurting anyone and helping many…

Other keys terms to this step are: Moderation, Efficiency, Resourcefulness, and Creativeness.

Integrity

Your integrity is part of your character. Character can be developed to provide the positive impression upon all those you meet and interact with. You do what you say you will do and you do it right the first time. People will soon recognize that you follow through on your commitments and that you are a person of strength, honesty, power, and trust. Further, this habit of following through with your obligations to yourself and others will drive you to be a very successful person. Moreover, avoiding things that are a waste of your time will benefit all persons as you will not engage things that do not improve all involved with your whole heart and mind.

Other keys terms to this step are: Honestly, Fearlessness, Purposefulness, and Invincibility.

System –Planning

Preparing for your goals is fundamental. Plan what you are going to do. Be very specific. Outline the steps needed and drive toward the desired outcome. Be prepared for outcomes that are as good as or even better than you desire. Know what you will do and prepare for any circumstance of importance. Be ready to act, engage, contemplate, and receive your good.

Other Keys to this Step are: Readiness, Accurateness, Utility, and Comprehensiveness.

Sympathy and Harmony

The ability to put yourself in the shoes of another will allow you to develop understanding of others. We do not know what other people are thinking or experiencing. Thus, we try to understand others goals and challenges. Let your kindness and gentleness be known. Speak and act with power, strength, grace and poise. Do not react to the world, RESPOND to it with Responsibility and treat others in the ways that you would want to be treated. Learn to communicate and receive opportunity by understanding what others are saying first.

Other keys terms to this step are: Kindness, Gentleness, Insight, Awareness, and Generosity.

Sincerity

Honesty is connected to truth. There is the truth that others speak, but more importantly, there is the truth of what we perceive and analyze. When we operate on this plane, we must try to perceive truth at the highest level. If you sincerely act and think in certain constructive ways, constructive opportunity will be attracted to you. As above, so below AND "Like attracts Like". You need not seek power over others, you give others the impression of increase and they will be attracted to your value, service, wisdom and quality of your living.

Other keys terms to this step are: Attractiveness, Power, and Simplicity

Impartiality

Sometimes the word impartial implies that we should not keep bias. This less bias that we hold in our preconceptions, the more harmony that we have with the world. Our minds must be open to receive from any channels of higher good that are provided.

Other keys terms to this pillar are: Justice, Patience, Wisdom, and Calmness

Self Reliance

You are to become rich in life. Spiritual Abundance is yours and it is your birthright. Your sixth sense becomes available to you through your connection to spiritual abundance and prosperity. You are connected and harmonized with the universe; thus, you are cooperating and co-creating with the world. You will become self reliant as you are moving closer to your true place which is utilizing your unique and creative abilities. Your true place is your right livelihood. Your "true place" IS your labor of love, and your work and efforts will be further harmonized to become a wealth of opportunity and abundance in your personal and working endeavors. Remain committed to your dreams & your true self so that your given talents will unfold and multiply.

Other keys terms to this step are: Decisiveness, Independence, Dignity, and Steadfastness.

- Interpreted and extracted from the works of James Allen – As a Man Thinketh 1902 and 8 Pillars of Prosperity 1911

Beatitudes: A Brief Analysis & Positive Meanings

The Beatitudes (Latin: beatitudo, happiness) is the name given to the best-known & introductory portion of the Sermon on the Mount of the Gospel of Matthew. For purposes of analyzing the mindset of abundance, we show each basic part of the Beatitudes and provide some insight into the highest meaning of each.

1.   **Poor in Spirit – Theirs is the Kingdom of Heaven** - This means that we should be teachable, be willing to grow. Humility is understanding your right size, putting the source of good first, and putting spirit before ego.

2.   **Mourn – They will be Comforted** - This implies that we should turn our will toward the Spirit. Understand your instincts and transcend the instincts that may result in destructive thinking and action.

3.   **The Meek – Shall Inherit the Earth** - Forgive, clean house, receive forgiveness. Through self analysis, meditation, or focused prayer and visualization, you can allow for the highest thoughts to enter your spiritual mind.

4.   **Those who Hunger – They will be filled.** - Remain hungry for insight and guidance. Never give up. The mind is connected to all and is a recipient of the greatest of wisdom if it is allowed to receive prosperous intelligence.

5.   **The Merciful – Will obtain Mercy** - Think and project love and gratitude. Radiate your good toward all including those who may have hurt you in the past. It is key for you to rise above past hurts and become the best you can be while also affording kind acts toward others that will help them grow.

6.   **The Pure in Heart – Will See God** - Our thinking, our actions and our omissions are part of our mind and character. Keeping a mind directed toward the highest good will always expand your good and flow of it toward you.

7.   **The Peacemakers – Will be the Children of God** - Bring Harmony, win-win relationships to all without facilitating injury toward yourself or family.

8.   **The Persecuted – Theirs in the Kingdom of Heaven** - Experience and feel: a catharsis, absolution, forgiveness, and wholeness. Keep in mind that the self can give the illusion of self persecution. Your duty is to transcend your mind with peace, love, abundance, and gratitude.

12 Steps of Abundance and Right Thinking with Scripture Comparison Notes on the Right.

Step 1: Admitted that ego and self is limited, and that living under this power of self and destructive thinking has resulted in a life of frustration without peace of mind.	I know that nothing good lives in me, that is, in my sinful nature. For I have the desire to do what is good, but I cannot carry it out. (Romans 7:18)
Step 2: Came to believe that the personal recognition of Spiritual abundance within my own being and without would allow prosperity in my life.	Jesus said unto him, If thou canst believe, all things are possible to him that believeth. And straightway the father of the child cried out, and said with tears, Lord, I believe; help thou mine unbelief. (Mark 9:23-24)
Step 3: Made a decision to seek Spirit before ego by seeking a harmonious relationship with the Universal Spirit Force of abundance.	If anyone would come after me, he must deny himself and take up his cross daily and follow me. (Luke 9:23**)
Step 4: I engage in self-analysis for the purpose of removing wasteful thought energy.	Let us examine our ways and test them, and let us return to the Lord. (Lamentations 3:40)
Step 5: I expose to my higher self and another human being the exact nature of the destructive thoughts and actions of the past.	Therefore confess your sins to each other and pray for each other so that you may be healed. (James 5:16)
Step 6: I became willing to have the Universal Spirit remove my destructive beliefs in favor of building my own character of goodness and prosperity.	If you are willing and obedient, you will eat the best from the land. (Isaiah 1:19)
Step 7: I humbly asked the Universal Spirit to remove my consciousness of fear, failure, poverty, or inadequacy.	Humble yourselves before the Lord, and He will lift you up. (James 4:10)

Step 8: I made a list of all relationships gone bad and became willing to allow the Universal Spirit mend my soul and heart and allow *my* forgiveness permanently.	Therefore, if you are offering your gift at the altar and there remember that your brother has something against you, leave your gift there in front of the altar. First go and be reconciled to your brother; then come and offer your gift. (Matthew 5:23, 24**)
Step 9: I allow the Universal Spirit to help me heal relationships wherever possible, except when to do so would create more harm than good to all parties involved.	Give and it shall be given you. A good measure, pressed down, shaken together and running over, will be poured into your lap. For with the measure you use, it will be measured to you. (Luke 6:38**)
Step 10: I continue to periodically analyze my thinking, and immediately recognize and correct error consciousness while avoiding destructive actions.	For by the grace given me I say to every one of you: Do not think of yourself more highly than you ought, but rather think of yourself with sober judgment, in accordance with the measure of faith GOD has given you. (Romans 12:3)
Step 11: I Seek to maintain a harmonious, grateful and thankful relationship with my inner self and with The Universal Spirit of abundance.	Let the word of Christ dwell in you richly. (Col. 3:16)
Step 12: Having become Spiritually awake as a result of these steps, I carried this message to others, and practiced these principles in my life affairs.	Brothers, if someone is caught in a sin, you who are Spiritual should restore him gently. But watch yourself, or you also may be tempted. Carry each other's burdens, and in this way you will fulfill the law of Christ. (Galatians 6:1-2)

Laws of Success – Edw. Beals - Ambition and Desire

Ambition what a glorious word! How the very sound of it stirs one's energies, and makes one feel the inspiration to be up and at work doing things, succeeding, creating, accomplishing! And what does ambition really mean, pray? It means more than a mere eagerness for things. It means the deep-seated desire to materialize certain ideals which exist in the mind as mental pictures. Before one can accomplish things, they must be possessed of Ambition. There is a psychological law underlying this mental hunger that manifests as Ambition. And the law is - that in order for the mental hunger to be manifested it must have ideals presented to the mind's eye. If you are contented with your present life, and want nothing better, it is chiefly because you know nothing better - have seen nothing better - have heard nothing better, or else you are mentally and physically lazy. An ignorant savage seeking to till his land by means of sharpened stick, cannot desire a steel plow or other agricultural implements if he does not know them. He simply keeps right at his work in his old way - the way of his forefathers - and feels no desire for a better implement. If he be a progressive savage, he begins to wish he had one of the strange new implements, and if he wants it hard enough he begins to experience a new, strange feeling of mental hunger for the thing, which if sufficiently strong, causes his ambition to bud.

And this is the critical point. Up to this time he has felt the strong desire preceding Ambition. But now with the dawn of Ambition comes the arousing of the Will. And this is what ambition is. A strong Will aroused by a Strong Desire or Purpose. To manifest Ambition fully, one must first eagerly desire the thing - not a mere "wanting" or "wishing" for it, but a fierce, eager, consuming hunger which demands satisfaction. And then one must have a Will aroused sufficiently strong to go out and get that which desire is demanding. There two elements constitute the activity of Ambition. The trouble with the majority of the people is that they have been taught that one should take what was given them and be content. But this is not nature's way. Nature implants in each living being a strong desire for which is necessary for its well-being and nourishment, and a strong will to gratify that natural desire.

There is no earthly reason why a person should not stimulate that fierce hunger for attainment by painting mental pictures of what they need. "But does this not arouse covetousness?" you may ask. Not at all - you are not coveting the things the others have, but merely desiring other things like them. You are willing that these other people should retain their things, but are demanding similar things for yourself. This is not covetousness, but laudable Ambition.

And laudable ambition is right. There are enough of the good things in this world for all of us, if we demand them, and reach out for them. Demand causes supply, in and under the LAW, so be not afraid. Arouse your ambition - it is a good thing and not something of which you should be ashamed. Urge it on - feed it - stimulate its growth. It is not a foul weed, but a strong, vigorous, healthy plant in the garden of life, bearing more fruit than any other growing thing there. Therefore, be not afraid to stand boldly out, crying: "I want this, and I am going to have it! It is the rightful heritage and I demand it of the LAW!" Be ambitious to attain Financial Success because that is the goal for which we are striving. Many persons seem afraid to speak desire, for they have gotten the term and idea mixed up with desires of an unworthy and detrimental nature. They have overlooked the fact that desire must underlie all human action - must be causing power back of and underneath Will itself.

You must not only "want" to do the thing, or to possess a thing, but you must "want to hard." You must want it as a hungry man wants bread, as the smothering man wants air. And if you will but arouse in yourself this fierce, ardent, insatiable desire, you will set in operation Nature's most potent mental forces.

Before we can manifest energy, there must be a strong impelling desire. Do not be afraid to allow your desire for Financial Success to burn brightly. Keep the ashes for past failures, disappointments, and discouragements well cleared away so that you may have a good draught. Keep the fire of desire burning brightly, ardently and consistently.

Do not be side tracked by outside things, for remember, concentrated desire is that which produces the greatest steam producing power. Keep your mind fixed on which you want, and keep on demanding that which belongs to you, for it is your own. The Universal Supply is adequate for all needs of everyone, but it responds only to the insistent demand and earnest desire. Learn to desire things in earnest, and rest not content with a mere wanting and wishing.

Desire creates Mental Attitude - develops Faith - nourishes ambition - unfolds Latent Powers - and tends directly and surely toward Success. Let the strong, dominant desire for Financial Independence possess you from the tips of your toes to the roots of your hair, - feel it surging through every part of your body - and then don't stop until you reach your goal.

Latent Powers

In this section, I recall the words Lovell: "There are infinite powers lying dormant in man, here, now - powers which, could he but catch a glimpse of, would endow his life on this planet with greater splendor, and impart to it a redoubled interest."

Nearly every man or woman who has attained success along any of the varied lines of human endeavor will tell you that at some period of their life they were called upon to assume certain responsibilities - undertake some unaccustomed task - play some unfamiliar part on life's stage - and then much to their surprise, found that they had within them the power, capability and qualifications for a successful accomplishment of the strange task. The crucial point was when they were brought face to face with the new undertaking. If, as in the case with the majority of people, they lacked nerve enough to say "I Can and I Will," the story was ended. But if they had that something within them which enabled them to assert their determination to face the thing manfully and at least to go down with their flags flying rather than to run away, they would find much to their surprise that there was within them a power which responded to the needs of the hour and which enabled them to master the undertaking. When asked "Can You?," instead of saying "On, no, I've never done that kind of work - it is impossible," they answered like the boy after the woodchuck; "I've just got to - I Can and I Will."

Is it merely a lesson in facing difficulties, and cultivating nerve and self-confidence? Not entirely - it teaches these things and also teaches the still greater truth that every man and woman has within themselves wonderful powers, lying dormant and unsuspected, which are merely awaiting the word of the master Will, impelled by a burning, eager, ardent desire, to spring at once into being, full armed and equipped for the fray.

And so my parting words for this essay are: Do not hesitate to accept any new responsibility, whether the same is forced upon you, or whether you reach out for it yourself. Say to yourself over and over again, "I can and I will accomplish this task. Talk with the successful people of the world, and they will tell you that they have had this experience over and over again. The demand always brings the supply, if we will but open ourselves to the inflow from the great Source of Supply - the Universal Power House.

Will Power

Tennyson well voices his human regard and admiration for the power of the Will. He tells us again, "O living Will, thou shalt endure, when all that seems shall suffer shock." The Will of man is a strange, subtle, intangible, and yet very real thing, that is closely connected with the inmost essence of his "I". When the "I" acts, it acts through the Will. The Will is the immediate expression of the EGO, or "I" in Man, which rests at the very seat of his being. This Ego, or "I" within each of us expresses itself in two ways. It first asserts "I Am," by which it expresses its existence and reality; then it asserts "I Will," by which it expresses its desire to act, and its determination to do so. The "I Will" comes right from the center of your being, and is the strongest expression of the Great Life Force within you, and in the degree that you cultivate and express it is the degree of positivity that you manifest.

The person of weak Will is a negative, cringing weakling, while he of strong Will is the positive, courageous, masterful individual in whom Nature delights and whom she rewards. The human Will is an actual living force. It is only when the necessity arises from some new unexpected demand for the exercise of the Will, that many people realize that they really possess such a Will. To many, alas, such a necessity never comes.

The man or woman with the strong Will knows when to recede from their position as well as when to go forward; they never stand still. When the occasion warrants it, they step back, but only for the purpose of getting a better start, for they always have a definite goal in view. The best way to do this is to first recognize your lack, and then by constant affirmations of "I can and I will accomplish this thing," and by the repetition of selections on the Will, taken from the best literature, build up within yourself, little by little, an invincible power and energy that will overcome every temptation that would side-track you from your life purpose.

First there comes that belief in ones ability, powers, and force which begets confidence, and which causes one to make a clear mental channel over which the Will flows.

Then, second, comes the assertion of the Will itself - the "I WILL" with all the force and energy and determination of the individual's character being poured into it, then does the Will become a very dynamic force which sweeps away obstacles before it in its mighty powers.

Look around you, and you will see the men and women of giant Wills set up a stronger center of influence, which extends on all sides and all directions, affecting this one and that one, and drawing and compelling others to fall in with the movements instigated by that Will or Energy.

Harmony

We should cultivate this habit in moments of mediation, when we may escape from the people and crowd, and thus be able to listen to the voice that sounds from within. Here are a few directions for entering into harmony with the Universal Rhythm of Force; first, your mental attitude must be right. You must have gained control of your thoughts and words, so that your mind is open and receptive to the great good of the world.

There must be no hate there, no discouragement, no pessimism, no negative, cringing, worm-of-the-dust or poverty thought--your frame of mind must be that of good will, encouragement, optimism, with positive thoughts, expectant of wealth, prosperity, and all of the good things that man, heir of the universe, is entitled to by right of his sonship. This latter mental attitude will surround you with a personal thought atmosphere which repels from you the negative or evil things and attracts you to the positive or good things of life.

Early in the morning just after your bath or shower, close the doors of your room, shutting out everybody and everything for just a few moments. Take precautions that you shall not be disturbed, and put away from your mind the fear of interruption and disturbance. Take a position of restful and peaceful calm. Relax every muscle, and take the tension off every nerve. Take a few deep restful breaths which will seem like sighs, and will tend to relax your body and mind. Then detach your thoughts from the outer world, the things, and turn the mind inward upon yourself. Shut out all the material cares, worries and problems of the day, and sink into a mental state of a peaceful calm. Think "I open myself to the inflow of the universal rhythmic harmony," and you will soon begin to feel a sense of relationship with that harmony coming into you, filling your mind and body with a feeling of rest and peace, and latent power. Then shortly after will come to you a sense of new strength and energy, and a desire to once more emerge upon the scene of your duties. This is the time for you to close your meditation.

Here it is; a few moments spent with your inner self and the Great Universal Power each day, as described above, if practiced assiduously, will establish within you the Create Mind--that wonderful thing which marks the difference between the ditch digger, who plods along from day to day with never a new idea for his own or humanity's betterment, and the man "at the top" who "does things;" the constructive man who builds railroads, steamships, large mercantile establishments.

The more you practice, the more you will open up that great subconscious reservoir of yours which is overflowing with original ideas. In time you will gain the power to get in touch with your inner self and tap that reservoir where ever you may be--in a car--out for a walk--while you are shaving--and there will be a flash through to your subconscious mind, in vivid outlines, ideas that when worked out will mean for you money and financial independence.

Creation

Did you ever think that the great buildings which rear their imposing forms and shapes along our business streets were created in the minds of their architects, and actually existed in their minds before the buildings could be erected? Anything and everything that has ever been created in material form must of necessity have been created in mental form previously. There is no exception to this rule. Everything that you can see, or think of, that has been made, has been first created mentally, in its every part and as a whole. And so it is with Financial Success. You must form a mental picture of what you want, and then bend every effort to fill in the picture.

Every person should have a purpose in life. To win anything in life one should have a definite goal for which to strive. We should have a picture in our mind of what we want to own or attain. If we want money, we should create a mental picture of money, see ourselves using it, handling it, spending it, acquiring more, and in short going through all the motions of the man of money. One should paint a great mental picture of wealth, and then start to work to fill in the picture, and materializo it.

And so it is with the majority of people--they sit down and say "oh, I want money--I want money," and that is all there is to it. They do not use their imaginations sufficiently to mentally create money, and then to proceed to materialize it.

Oh, I tell you friends, you must first know just what you want, before you will be able to materialize it. Unless you know what you want, you will never get anything. The great successful men of the world have used their imaginations, instead of despising them. They think ahead and create their mental picture, and then go to work materializing that picture in all its details, filling in here, adding in there, altering this a bit and that a bit, but steadily building--steadily building.

Concentration

What is concentration? Well, the dictionaries tell us that the word means the act or process of bringing and directing things toward a common center, and thereby condensing and intensifying the force of the thing. And that is the key-note of the word - that is the mental picture of it - this directing of forces in a common center.

We can never expect to win out in anything unless we firmly concentrate our minds upon the thing we seek. We have got to make our mental picture of what we want, and then start to desire it as hard as we are able to, and by doing so we will concentrate our attention and will upon that thing until "something happens." We must learn to concentrate our powers and will upon the desired object, just as the sun-glass concentrates the rays of the sun upon the common focus. We must learn to focus our energies upon the thing we want, and then keep the focus steady from day to day, never allowing ourselves to be side-tracked or swerved from our main object of desire, interest and will. One should begin practicing concentration on little things, until one masters them, and then he or she may move on to the consideration and contemplation of larger things. It is quite an art to be able to do one thing at a time, to the exclusion of distracting thoughts and objects. The best workmen along any line of human effort are those who are able to concentrate on their work, and practically lose themselves in their tasks for the time being.

The first step in acquiring Concentration begins, of course, in the control of the attention. Master the attention and you have acquired the art of Concentration. By holding your attention upon a thing, you direct it to your mental forces, and new ideas, plans and combinations spring into your mind and fly to a common center. Besides this you put into operation the Law of Attraction and direct its forces to that same common center. Without concentrated attention you scatter and dissipate your mental forces and accomplish nothing at all. I urge upon all who read this book the importance of beginning to cultivate concentration. Begin by acquiring the habit of attending to one thing at a time, concentrating the attention upon it, and then completing it and passing on to another thing.

Avoid the baneful practice of thinking of one thing while doing another. Think of and work upon the thing before you, and hold your attention there until it is completed. The thinking and action should pull together, instead of in opposite directions. The eminent authorities tells us that; "It is a matter of no small importance that we acquire the habit of doing only one thing at a time, by which I mean that while attending to any one object, our thoughts ought not to wander to another." The celebrated Lord Chesterfield said; "There is time enough for everything in the course of a day, if you do but one thing at a time; but there is not time enough in a year, for you to do two things at a time." If there is any secret of concentration, it is contained in that sentence. You can concentrate on anything you are intensively interested in, or dearly love. For instance, if you are a young man engaged to a beautiful young lady (the ideal soul mate to make your life complete) you have no trouble in thinking about her and how happy you will be after the knot is tied. In fact, most of your time - when you are not thinking of your work - is given over to the thought of that girl, and your future together.

And we might go down the whole gamut of humanity and find some one thing which each person is interested in or loves, and we would soon see that it is not a hard task for a person to think about or concentrate on that which is most dear to him or her. For with money at your disposal you can give that girl everything she needs to make her happy; you can ensure that child's future and make sure that it has the education which it deserves; you can establish that boy in business and give him a chance to express his full ability; you can complete those plans you've had in mind for so long and you can do many things which are now impossible.

When you find yourself thinking of something foolish, exert your will, draw back your thoughts, use your imagination to picture an ideal of what Financial Independence will mean to you, and then concentrate your whole thought on that ideal to bring it into materialization.

Persistence and Habit

What is needed is a steady, determined, persistent application to the one object upon which you have set your mind. There is nothing like sticking to a thing. Many men are brilliant, resourceful, and industrious, but they fail to reach the goal by reason of their lack of "stick-to-it-iveness." One should acquire the tenacity of a bulldog, and refuse to be shaken off of a thing once he has fixed his attention and desire upon it.

No matter how strong a Will a person may have, if they have not learned the art of persistent application of it they fail to obtain the best results. One must acquire that constant, unvarying, unrelenting application to the object of one's Desire that will enable them to hold their Will firmly against the object until it is shaped according to their wishes. Not only today and tomorrow, but every day until the end, Abraham Lincoln said of General Grant: "The great thing about him is the cool persistency of purpose. He is not easily excited, and he has got the grip of a bulldog. When he once gets his teeth in, nothing can shake him off."

The Will is the hard chisel, but Persistence is the mechanism that holds the chisel in its place firmly pressing it up against the object to be shaped, and keeping it from slipping or relaxing its pressure. If you lack Persistence, you should begin to train yourself in the direction of acquiring the habit if sticking to things. This practice will establish a new habit of mind, and will also tend to cause the appropriate brain cells to develop and thus give to you as a permanent characteristic the desired quality you are seeking to develop. Fix your mind upon your daily tasks, studies, occupation or hobbies, and hold your attention firmly upon them by Concentration, until you find yourself getting into the habit of resisting "side-tracking" or distracting influences. Persistence and rest will follow naturally as the fruit allows the budding and flowering of the tree.

If it be true that Habit becomes a cruel tyrant ruling and compelling men against their will, desire, and inclination--and this is true in many cases, the question naturally arises in the thinking mind whether this mighty force can be harnessed and controlled in the service of man, just as have other forces of Nature. If this result can be accomplished, the man may master Habit and set it to work, instead of being a slave to it.

A habit is a "mental path" over which our actions have traveled for some time, each passing making the path a little deeper and a little wider. It is movement along the lines of the least resistance--passage over the well worn path.

As an instance of the latter, it is pointed out that a piece of paper once folded in a certain manner will fold along the same lines next time. And, remember this always--the best (and one might say the only) way in which old habits may be removed is to form new habits to counteract and replace the old undesirable ones.

Form new mental paths over which to travel and the old ones will soon become less distinct and with time practically fill up from disuse. Every time you travel over the path of the desirable mental habit, you make the path deeper and wider and make it so much easier to travel thereafter. This mental path-making is a very important thing, and I cannot urge upon you too strongly the injunction to start to work making the desirable mental path over which you wish to travel. Practice, practice, practice--be a good path-maker.

George Mentz, JD, MBA

Claiming Your Own

There has grown up in the minds of many people the delusion that there is some real merit in taking the mental position that desirable things are "too good for me," and denying if they have any merit whatsoever in them. So prevalent has become this idea that it has developed a race of hypocrites and Pharisees, who go out proclaiming their humble goodness, and their meek humility, until one gets tired of hearing their talk--and talk is all there is to it, for these people slyly manage to reach out for the good things in sight, even while decrying the value of the aforesaid good things, and denying their worthiness to receive anything at all. I take quite the other position. I believe that there is nothing too good for the men and women who assert their right to live and to partake of the good thing of earth.

Napoleon understood human nature and the laws of psychology. Tell a man that he is a worm of the dust and is deserving of nothing but kicks and punishment, and if he believes you he will sink to the mental level of a worm and will cringe and crawl and eat dirt. But let him know that he has within him the divine spark, and that there is nothing too good for him; nothing that he has not a right to aspire to-- tell him these things, I say, and he will become a transfigured creature, ready and willing to attempt great things and do mighty deeds.

"As a man thinketh in his heart so is he." And this is why I am trying to tell you that you have a right to all the good things there are--that you are a worthy thing and not a crawling thing in the dust. That is why I tell you to raise up your head and look the world in the eyes affirming your relationship with the Divine Cause that brought you into being, and asserting your right to partake of your heritage from that power.

The very persons who hold up this weak, negative ideal to their followers are not especially noted for their meekness or humility--they are apt to be arrogant, selfish, and grasping of all good things in sight, even while decrying and denying them. Away with such destructive and hurtful teachings of "can't phrases" and negative emotions. Make way for the new teaching that the good things of earth have been placed here for man's use, and for his development and happiness. There is nothing too good for Men of Women, for they are the rightful inheritors and heirs of the Universal Supply.

Does not nature seem to strive to produce strong plants, strong animals, and strong individuals? Does she not seem to delight in producing an individual, in either of the great kingdoms of life, who has the desire, energy, ambition, and power to draw to itself the nourishment and nutriment which will enable it to express its life fully--which will enable it to become a proper, efficient, and worthy channel through which may flow the great Stream of Life that has its source in the Divine Cause which is behind and back of all things? Is life an effort to produce weak, miserable, unhappy beings--or is it an urge that seeks to develop strong, happy, noble, individual forms?

These people would even deny the supply. Oh, I say to you, friends, the power that called us into being has placed in this world of ours all that is necessary to our well-being and has implanted in our breasts the natural hunger for nourishment, physical, mental, and spiritual. This very hunger is nature's promise that there exists that which is intended to satisfy it. And then, what folly to decry hunger, or to deny supply. That which you need and for which you are hungry, exists for you. It is yours, and you are not robbing others when you seek for it and draw it to you.

George Mentz, JD, MBA

Fear and Worry

Fear and the emotions that come from its being do more to paralyze useful effort, good work, and finely thought-out plans than anything else known to man. It is the great hobgoblin of the race. It has ruined the lives of thousands of people. It has destroyed the finely budding characters of men and woman, and made negative individuals of them in the place of strong, reliant, courageous doers of useful things. Worry is the oldest child of fear. The majority of things we fear and worry about never come to pass at all, and the few that do actually materialize are never as bad as we feared they would be. You will learn what it is to have a mind cleared of weeds, and fresh to grow healthy thoughts, feelings, emotions, and ambitions.

You will find that when you are rid of fear, you will radiate hope, and confidence, and ability, and will impress all those with whom you come in contact. When one fears a thing, then they may really attracts it to themselves, just as if they desired it. The reason is this - when one desires or fears a thing (in either case the principle is the same) he or she creates a mental picture of the thing, which mental picture has a tendency toward materialization. With this mental picture in their mind - if they hold to it long enough - they draw the things or conditions to them, and thus "thought takes form in action and being." The majority of out fears and worries are silly little things that take our thought for a moment, and then are gone. They are great wasters of energy, but we do not concentrate on any one of them long enough to put into operation the Law of Attraction.

"But how may I kill it out?" You cry. Very easily! This is the method: Suppose you had a roomful of darkness. Would you start to shovel or sweep out the darkness? Or would you throw open the window and admit the light? When the light pours in, the darkness disappears. And so, with the darkness of Fear - throw open the windows, and "let a little sunshine in." Let the thoughts, feelings, and ideals of courage, confidence, and fearlessness pour into your mind, and fear will vanish. Whenever fear shows itself in your mind, administer the antidote of Fearlessness immediately. Say to yourself; "I am fearless; I fear nothing; I am courageous," Let the sunshine pour in. To those who understand the LAW.

The Secrets Decoded

Faith is the process which one raises to meet the Great Forces of Life and Nature, and by means of which is behind, and in all things, and is enabled to apply that Power to the running of their own affairs. To some, it may seem a far cry from Faith to Financial Success, but to those who have demonstrated the truths enunciated in this little book, the two are closely interwoven.

For one to attain Success they must first have faith in themselves; second, faith in their fellowman; and third, faith in the LAW. Faith in oneself is of primary importance, for unless one has it, they can never accomplish anything; can never influence any other person's opinion of them, can never attract to themselves the things, persons and circumstances necessary for their welfare. A person must first learn to believe in themselves before they will be able to make others believe in them. But, if you let pour forth a full, abiding, confident faith in yourself, your abilities, your qualities, your latent powers, your desires, your plans, your success; in short, you will find the whole mental garden responds to the stimulating influence; and ideas, thoughts, plans, and other mental flowers will spring up rapidly. There is nothing so stimulating as a strong, positive "I Can and I Will" attitude toward oneself.

And you remember what has been said about the Law of Attraction - you remember how "like attracts like." and how one's Mental Attitude tends to draw toward them the things in harmony with his or her thoughts. Well, this being so, can you not see that a Mental Attitude of Faith of Confidence in oneself is calculated to attract to you that which fits in with such Faith - that will tend to materialize your idea? You must have confidence in a person before you care to deal with them. It is much better to maintain the thought of good-will, fellowship, and confidence towards one's fellowman, weighing all things impartially from an unprejudiced standpoint and then render your decision after due thought from the facts in the case. But, by all means, have faith in your fellowman.

You will note that nearly all successful men and women have a deep-rooted belief in Something Outside that helps them along. You manifest faith at every turn of the road. And this being so, why should you not manifest faith in the underlying LAW which is manifesting in things?

Auto Suggestion

You will have noticed that in the preceding chapters I have begun a serious campaign in the direction of having you "make yourself over" mentally, in order to bring you under the operation of the Law of Financial Success and Spiritual Abundance.

1. You will remember that first we tried to get you to regard Limitless

Abundance and Money in a new light - as a natural supply akin to the

nourishment of the plant, and coming under the same general law of

Natural Supply and Demand.

2. We urged you to build up the proper Mental Attitude, showing you

how by so doing you would cultivate within yourself the faculties,

qualities and powers conducive to success; the qualities likely to

attract and influence people with whom you come in contact; and the

mental state which would set into operation the beneficent phases of

the Law of Attraction.

3. We preceded to explain how to rid Fear and Worry from of your

mental system.

4. We stated strategies that would help you cultivate the quality of your Faith.

5. We covered the consideration of the Latent Powers and the rules for their unfoldment.

6. We explained of the nature of Ambition, and the urge to cultivate and develop it.

7. We summarized the concept of the wonderful effect of Desire, and the steps to cultivate Desire as the means of cultivating Will.

8. We showed the importance of the development of a powerful Will, the acquirement of which means so much to you.

Now if you will stop a moment, you will see that the practical application of the instruction given and the precepts laid down for your guidance require a certain "making over" of yourself, on your part. In the first place the term "suggestion," as used by psychologists means "an impression made upon the mind of another." And in "auto-suggestion" is an impression made upon ones own mind in a manner similar to that used in impressing the mind of another. You will see this a little clearer in a moment. The whole essence of Suggestion lies in the idea of "impression."

Suggestion is not a matter of argumentative effort, but a process of saying a thing so positively, earnestly, and convincingly that the other person takes up the idea without argument. Not only should one "affirm" things to oneself, but should also create Mental Images of the desired thing, and should also act out the part he or she wishes to play, in a sort of extended preliminary rehearsal. The thing to remember is that constant thinking of a desired quality of mind, accompanied with the indulgence in the Mental Pictures of yourself as actually possessed of the quality itself, and also accompanied by an "acting out" of the part you would like to play, will in due time so impress and mold your mind that you will actually possess the quality itself. Here is a great psychological law I have expressed. Read it again, study it, and make it your own.

For instance, let us suppose you lack Ambition. Well, the first thing is to arouse the Desire to become Ambitious. Then start in the plan to make constant affirmation to the fact that; "I am Ambitious--very Ambitious--my Ambition grows everyday," and so on. Then, picture yourself in your imagination as being Ambitious--see yourself as moving around the world possessed of an insatiable Ambition which is leading you to a effective action and wonderful accomplishments.

Then begin to act out the part of the Ambitious man or woman. Study some Ambitious man until you catch his feelings and then begin to look Ambitious; talk in the tone of a man possessing Ambition; walk like an Ambitious man--in short act out the part to the smallest details. I do not mean to copy the mannerisms of the man you have taken for your model--this is not the thing at all.

Simply study him until you get his feelings--until you can recognize the Ambitious emotion and Mental Attitude animating him, and then go to work to feel the same inward feeling yourself, and to act out the feeling. If you can once get the feeling; then, all you have got to do is act it out right.

Summary of The Laws of Success – Mentz Edw. Beales revised from 1907 Anonymous Book

The Secrets Decoded

Spiritual Connection of Abundance

Without a doubt, the spiritual connection to your higher path, your higher power or your higher self is what will allow for the most simple flow of abundance in your life. We can't tell you exactly what will get you connected to the source, but we can say this, "If you acquire a harmonious relation with the universal mind and source of energy, abundance will come to you much-much easier.

Engaging and being willing to achieve this connection to harmonious abundance should be your goal. Thy to develop an "All is Right with My World Attitude". You want to improve your conscious connection to your higher self to be your best. Having a bitter heart while attempting this may be difficult. Thus, see a life coach, analyst, psychologist, priest, confident, or counselor to work on issues that keep you in a disconnected mindset. Remember, your goal is to improve your character and to have a harmonious relationship with yourself, others and your higher self.

With this in mind, it is important to remember this. " In all probabilities, God does not exlst for those who repudiate the idea. For those open to the concept, the force and the energy of the spirit become real. Deny the Supernatural and there will be none. Reject miracles and they will escape you. Embrace the Universe and it will love and protect you in return."

With this supernatural connection to harmonious abundance, you will go from: Simply trying to avoid problems, to "getting by" effectively, to managing life with the ability to respond to it, to creation growth & change. Over time, you will evolve to a spiritual being who can co-create your life and future..

Some Concluding Observations – Wattles - Mentz

Many people will scoff at the idea that there is an exact science of spiritual abundance and wealth consciousness. Holding the impression that the supply of wealth is limited, they will insist that social and governmental institutions must be changed before even any considerable number of people can acquire a competence.

But this is not true. It is true that existing governments keep the masses in poverty, but this is because the masses do not think and act in the way of constructive prosperity.

If the masses were to begin to move forward as suggested in this book, neither governments nor industrial systems can stop them; all systems would need be modified to accommodate the forward movement. If the people have the advancing mind, have the faith that they can have a rich and full life, and move forward with the fixed purpose to attain wealth, nothing can possibly keep them in poverty.

Individuals may enter into the certain path at any time and under any government and make themselves rich. And when any considerable number of individuals do so under any government, they will cause the system to be so modified as to open the way for others. The more people who get rich on the competitive plane, the worse for others. The more who get rich on the creative plane, the better for others. Creation of new products, solutions, and cures always improves the whole.

For the present, however, it is enough to know that neither the government under which you live nor the capitalistic or competitive system of industry can keep you from wealth. When you enter upon the creative and constructive plane of thought you will rise above all these things and become a citizen of another kingdom.

But remember that your thought must be held upon the creative plane. You are never for an instant to be betrayed into regarding the supply as limited or into acting on the moral level of competition. Whenever you do fall into old ways of thought, correct yourself instantly. For when you are in the competitive mind, you have lost the cooperation of the supreme mind.

Do not spend any time in planning as to how you will meet possible emergencies in the future, except as the necessary policies may affect your actions today. You are concerned with doing today's work in a perfectly successful manner and not with possible matters which may arise tomorrow. You can attend to them as they come. Do not concern yourself with questions as to how you shall surmount obstacles which may loom upon your business horizon unless you can see plainly that your course must be altered today in order to avoid or prepare for them. No matter how tremendous an obstruction may appear at a distance, you will find that if you go on in the path of abundance it will disappear as you approach it, or that a way over, under, through, or around it will appear. No possible combination of circumstances can defeat a man or woman who is proceeding to wealth along strictly spiritual and scientific lines. No man or woman who obeys the law can fail to improve; any more than one can multiply two by two and fail to get four.

Give no anxious thought to possible disasters, obstacles, panics, or unfavorable combinations of circumstances. There is time enough to meet such things when they present themselves before you in the immediate present, and you will find that every difficulty carries with it the wherewithal for its overcoming. Guard your speech. Never speak of yourself, your affairs, or of anything else in a discouraged or discouraging way. Never admit the possibility of failure or speak in a way that infers failure as a possibility.

Never speak of the times as being hard or of business conditions as being doubtful. Times may be hard and business doubtful for those who are on the competitive plane, but they can never be so for you. You can create what you want, and you are above fear. When others are having hard times and poor business, you will find your greatest opportunities.

George Mentz, JD, MBA

Train yourself to think of and to look upon the world as a something which is growing, and to regard seeming evil as being only that which is undeveloped. Always speak in terms of advancement. To do otherwise is to deny your faith, and to deny your faith is to lose it.

Never allow yourself to feel disappointed. You may expect to have a certain thing at a certain time and not get it at that time, and this will appear to you like failure. But if you hold to your faith you will find that the failure is only apparent. Continue on this abundant path, and if you do not receive that thing, you will receive something so much better that you will see that the seeming failure was really a great success.

A student of this science had set his mind on making a certain business combination which seemed to him at the time to be very desirable, and he worked for some weeks to bring it about. When the crucial time came, the thing failed in a perfectly inexplicable way. It was as if some unseen influence had been working secretly against him. But he was not disappointed. On the contrary, he thanked God that his desire had been overruled, and went steadily on with a grateful mind. In a few weeks an opportunity so much better came his way that he would not have made the first deal on any account, and he saw that a mind which knew more than he knew had prevented him from losing the greater good by entangling himself with the lesser.

That is the way every seeming failure will work out for you, if you keep your faith, hold to your purpose, have gratitude, and do each day all that can be done that day, doing each separate act in a successful manner. When you make a failure, it is because you have not asked for enough. Keep on, and a larger thing then you were seeking will certainly come to you. Remember this. You will not fail because you lack the necessary talent to do what you wish to do. If you go on as I have directed, you will develop all the talent that is necessary to the doing of your work.

However, do not hesitate or waver for fear that when you come to any certain place you will fail for lack of ability. Keep right on, and when you come to that place, the ability will be furnished to you. The same source of ability which enabled the untaught Lincoln to do the greatest work in government ever accomplished by a single man is open to you. You may draw upon all the mind there is for wisdom to use in meeting the responsibilities which are laid upon you. Go on in full faith.

As noted, "a person can form things in his thought, and, by impressing his thought upon formless substance, can cause the thing he thinks about to be created. In order to do this, a person must pass from the competitive to the creative mind; he must form a clear mental picture of the things he wants, and hold this picture in his thoughts with the fixed purpose to get what he wants, and the unwavering faith that he does get what he wants, closing his mind against all that may tend to shake his purpose, dim his vision, or quench his faith."

"A person may come into full harmony with the formless substance and spiritual abundance by entertaining a lively and sincere gratitude for the blessings it bestows upon him. Gratitude unifies the mind of man with the intelligence of substance, so that man's thoughts are received by the formless. A person can remain upon the creative plane only by uniting himself with the formless intelligence through a deep and continuous SINCERE feeling of gratitude."

Study this book. Make it your constant companion until you have mastered all the ideas contained in it. While you are getting firmly established in this faith, you will do well to give up most recreations and pleasure and to stay away from places where ideas conflicting with these are advanced in lectures or sermons. Do not read pessimistic or conflicting literature or get into arguments upon the matter.   Spend most of your leisure time in contemplating your vision, in cultivating gratitude, and in reading this book. It contains all you need to know of the science of abundance and spiritual wealth.
Wallace D. Wattles (1910) – Enhanced by Prof. Mentz

Special Exercises and Journal Writing

Buy a cheap notebook and have a pen ready. Here are some written exercises for growth and suggested questions for you to try to answer. Be proud of yourself for completing this book and attempting these exercises.

1. If you could not fail, what would you do with your life in your work, financial life, or relationships?
2. Write down as many accomplishments that you have been successful with. Begin with a diploma you received, a good job with family or work, or any job that you done.
3. Write down who you think you are: Example: I am a good parent, I am of Irish decent, I am a Spiritual Person. Etc.
4. Write down some ways in which you honor and respect yourself. Example: I go to the gym and eat right etc.
5. Write down some ways that you may pamper yourself. Example: Long Bath, Read Books, Play Sports, Quality time with loved ones etc.
6. Write down your 10 favorite types of labor that you enjoy that you consider fun. Example: Working with people, travel related jobs, creating things etc.
7. Write down 10 things you could do that would dramatically improve you life. Keep this list open to addition and subtraction.
8. Write down 10-20 attributes about yourself or things that you are thankful for. Keep this list open to addition.
9. Write down 10 things that you like to do or would like to do to enjoy life more. Examples: Movies, Reading, Bowling, Travel
10. Take out your resume and update it. Don't be shy and add to your resume anything that you have done for yourself, the community, your job, or any skills that you may have learned.
11. Write out a list of your creative ideas. What would you like to start, build, create, or solve.
12. Who are your favorite authors? Why? Did they inspire you?
13. Write out an appreciation list? Name the people who have helped you in your life? Honor them with a blessing.
14. Write out things you like about yourself and your best qualities.

15. What can you do to become a better listener and hear what others are saying to us.
16. What can you do to obtain greater peace of mind? How can we limit resentments, anger, and conflict while also protecting ourselves from any attack or abuse?
17. What can you do to become better prepared for life, success, financial challenges, educational or skills advancement, and self respect?
18. How can we learn better to communicate with others and also discuss our dreams and plans?
19. How can we be more attractive, more loving, more compassionate, & more helpful without doing more harm than good.
20. What calculated risks do you fear that would really benefit you and maybe your family. Example: Going back to school.
21. What can you do to better develop a harmonious relationship with yourself, your own ego, your higher self, the universe or GOD.
22. What can we do to better cultivate a thankful heart and a mind of more constructive thoughts.
23. What can we do to further develop our character and integrity.
24. If you could live or travel anywhere in the world, where would it be? Why? What would you do there?
25. Is there anyone in the world who really deserves an apology from you? Why? Would it help? Ask your spiritual counselor before taking this step any further.
26. Is there anyone in the world that you still hate? Could you pray for them once a day for 30 days? Why or Why Not? If this guaranteed relief, would you be willing to try.
27. Are you willing to honestly discuss your faults, strengths, and hopes with another person? Why? Or Why Not? If this would help you grow into a better person, can you try?
28. Are you willing to give more than is required in service, value, and quality?
29. Are you willing to keep a written list of several things to do each day toward your dreams? Can you try to do a few things effectively each day toward your ideals?

George Mentz, JD, MBA

Thoughts on Visualization Techniques

1. In a quiet spot, enter your relaxed state of mind and take a few deep breaths.
2. Relax each part of the body - one by one.
3. Close your eyes and imagine a snapshot picture of something that you really want to happen in your life.
4. Detail the final result of this wish using colors and 5 senses.
5. Imagine the emotions that you would have when this dream or goal or result is reached. FEEL the emotions of joy and thankfulness.
6. Harvest the mental essence of how having the result or thing will function in your life, serve you, and help all involved.
7. Believe that it has happened in your mind and allow yourself to imagine the ownership of this result mentally.
8. Pinpoint and focus on the completed final event of success. i.e. The foot race is completed OR the check is in your bank account.
9. Experience love and grateful feelings when you recognize and realize your vision. Know and Feel it "AS IF" it is FACT.
10. Imagine the benefits for all involved.
11. Be willing to receive all of this good on a mental and spiritual level which allows you to take actions toward creation and receiving the results
12. Make sure you have created ways to capture the result. Example: You may not be able to become the highest paid pilot without a license.
13. Send this mental vision into the world with joy as a "thought centered" letter to the supreme architect.
14. Respond to communication from others and your messages of intuition that come to you. Be willing to meet others half way and go the extra mile.
15. Allow your dreams to unfold on parallel lines. Example: You may want a successful business in selling this one thing, but the laws of attraction may allow you to sell many other things related to it.

Summary Of The Science Of Being Great – Wattles Mentz

We are made of the one intelligent substance, and therefore all contain the same essential powers and possibilities. Greatness is equally inherent in all, and may be manifested by all. Every person may become great. Many of the highest constituents of the Supreme Intelligence are also the constituents of man. We must learn to tap into these unused and latent spiritual powers.

We may overcome both heredity and circumstances by exercising the inherent creative power of the soul. If we are to become great, the soul must act, and must rule the mind and the body over the simple ego thoughts. Our knowledge is limited, and we fall into error through spiritual ignorance. To avoid this illusion and unawareness, we must connect our soul with Universal Spirit. Universal Spirit is the intelligent substance from which all things come. It is in and through all things. All things are known to this universal mind, and we can so unite ourselves with it as to enter into spirit and higher knowledge.

To do this we must cast out of ourselves everything that separates us from the Supreme. We must will to live the divine and abundant life, and we must rise above all simple, moral temptations. The seeker of spiritual abundance must forsake, repudiate, or transcend every course of action that is not in accord with our highest ideals.

We must reach the right viewpoint, recognizing that God is all, in all, and that there is nothing wrong. We must see that nature, society, government, and industry are perfect in their present stage, and advancing toward completion; and that all men and women everywhere are good and perfect. We must know that all is right with the world, and unite with God for the engagement of the perfect work. It is only as we see God as the Great Advancing Presence in all, and good in all that we can shift to real greatness.

The seeker must consecrate themselves to the service of the highest that is within, obeying the voice of the soul. There is an Inner Light in everyone that continuously impels us toward the highest, and we must be guided by this light if we would become great.

We must recognize the fact that we are one with the Father, and consciously affirm this unity for ourselves and for all others. We must know ourselves to be a "child of God" among "children of God", and act accordingly. We must have absolute faith in our own perceptions of truth, and begin at home to act upon these perceptions. As we see the true and right course in small things and actions, we must take that course. We must cease to act unthinkingly, and begin to think; and we must be sincere and honest in our thought.

We must form a mental conception of ourselves at the highest, and hold this conception until it is our habitual thought-form of ourselves. This thought-form we must keep continuously in view. We must outwardly realize and express that thought-form in our actions. We must do everything that we do in a great way. In dealing with our family, neighbors, acquaintances, and friends, we must make every act an expression of our ideals or highest good.

The person who reaches the right viewpoint and makes full consecration, and who fully idealizes their self as great, and who makes every act, however trivial, an expression of the ideal, has already attained to greatness. Everything we do will be done in a great way. We will make ourselves known, and will be recognized as a personality of power. We will receive knowledge by inspiration, and will know all that we need to know. We will receive all the material wealth we form in our thoughts, and will not lack for any good thing. We will be given ability to deal with any combination of circumstances that may arise, and our growth and progress will be continuous and rapid.

Some Classic Quotes

"We may divide thinkers into those who think for themselves and those who think through others. The latter are the rule and the former the exception. The first are original thinkers in a double sense, and egotists in the noblest meaning of the word." -Schopenhauer.

"The key to every man is his thought. Sturdy and defiant though he look he has a helm which he obeys, which is the idea after which all his facts are classified. He can only be reformed by showing him a new idea which commands his own." -Emerson.

"All truly wise thoughts have been thought already thousands of times; but to make them really ours we must think them over again honestly till they take root in our personal expression." -Goethe.

"All that a man is outwardly is but the expression and completion of his inward thought. To work effectively he must think clearly. To act nobly he must think nobly." -Channing.

"Great men are they who see that spirituality is stronger than any material force; that thoughts rule the world." -Emerson.

"Some people study all their lives, and at their death they have learned everything except to think." -Domergue.

"It is the habitual thought that frames itself into our life. It affects us even more than our intimate social relations do. Our confidential friends have not so much to do in shaping our lives as the thoughts have which we harbor?' -J. W. Teal.

"When God lets loose a great thinker on this planet, then all things are at risk. There is not a piece of science but its flank may be turned tomorrow; nor any literary reputation or the so-called eternal names of fame that may not be refused and condemned." -Emerson. Think! Think!! THINK!!! Wallace Wattes 1910

"All that we are is a result of what we have thought" - Buddha

R. W. Emerson – Thoughts on Self Reliance

There is a time in every man's education when he arrives at the conviction that envy is ignorance; that imitation is suicide; that he must take himself for better for worse as his portion; that though the wide universe is full of good, no kernel of nourishing corn can come to him but through his toil bestowed on that plot of ground which is given to him to till. The power which resides in him is new in nature, and none but he knows what that is which he can do, nor does he know until he has tried. Not for nothing one face, one character, one fact, makes much impression on him, and another none. This sculpture in the memory is not without pre-established harmony. The eye was placed where one ray should fall, that it might testify of that particular ray. We but half express ourselves, and are ashamed of that divine idea which each of us represents. It may be safely trusted as proportionate and of good issues, so it be faithfully imparted, but God will not have his work made manifest by cowards. A man is relieved and gay when he has put his heart into his work and done his best; but what he has said or done otherwise shall give him no peace. It is a deliverance which does not deliver. In the attempt his genius deserts him; no muse befriends; no invention, no hope.

Trust thyself: every heart vibrates to that iron string. Accept the place the divine providence has found for you, the society of your contemporaries, the connection of events. Great men have always done so, and confided themselves childlike to the genius of their age, betraying their perception that the absolutely trustworthy was seated at their heart, working through their hands, predominating in all their being. And we are now men, and must accept in the highest mind the same transcendent destiny; and not minors and invalids in a protected corner, not cowards fleeing before a revolution, but guides, redeemers and benefactors, obeying the Almighty effort and advancing on Chaos and the Dark.

Thoughts on Scripture – Classic Laws of Thought

To many, Scripture may not come to mind with daily challenges. However, once we have reflected on the ancient and proven teachings of these Transformational Teachings, we see that the keys to having an effective spiritual life are available for our growth.

We I think of lack or limitation, I now think of the Teachings of "**Laws of Abundance**" **John 10:10** "The thief comes only to steal and kill and destroy; I have come that they might have life, and that they might have it more abundantly.

When I worry about my perception and the truth, I can reflect on the "**Law of Thought**" **Matthew 6:22** "The **eye** is the **lamp** of the body. If your **eye**s are good, your whole body will be full of light.

When I want to procrastinate, I can remember the "**Law of Action**" and take steps each day toward improving my body, mind and spirit. **Luke 9:62** Jesus replied, "No one who puts his hand to the plow and looks back is fit for service in the kingdom of God."

When I have annoying thoughts, I can consider the "**Law of Love**" **Matthew 22: 36** Jesus replied: " 'I ove the Lord your God with all your heart and with all your soul and with all your mind.'[b] 38This is the first and greatest commandment. 39 And the second is like it: 'Love your neighbor as yourself.'[c] 40 All the Law and the Prophets hang on these two commandments."

When I wonder about my capabilities and ability to serve, The "**Law of Success**" must be pondered. **John 14:12** "The works that I do shall he do also; and greater works than these shall he do."

When I want to react or become overly attached to a situation instead of being still, walking away, or responding in spiritual manner, the " **Law of Non Resistance**" comes to mind. **Matthew 5:39** *Resist not Evil....*

When I wonder about the government and authority, I recall the "Law of Obedience" **Mark 12:17** "Give to Caesar what is Caesar's, and to God what is God's." I then realize that my spiritual life transcends over politics.

When I am harboring anger or resentment, I try to observe the "Law of Forgiveness" and the freedom that I receive by giving forgiveness, praying for others, and allowing myself to be forgiven. **Luke 6:37** [*Judging Others*] "Do not judge, and you will not be judged. Do not condemn, and you will not be condemned. **Forgive**, and you will be **forgiven**.

When I wonder if things will improve, I must give credence to the "Law of Increase" and to consider helping others and serving humanity. **Luke 6:38** Give, and it will be given to you. A good measure, pressed down, shaken together and running over, will be poured into your lap. For with the measure you use, it will be measured to you."

When I feel unworthy, I should observe the "**Law of Receiving**" and become open to receiving and having a blessed life. **Luke 16:12** "And if you have not been trustworthy with someone else's property, who will give you property of your own?"

When I feel lazy or unmotivated, the "**Law of Compensation**" often comes to mind and I try a little harder to plant good seeds of work into the world. **Galatians 6:7** "For whatsoever a man soweth, that shall he also **reap**.

When I don't feel like preparing or becoming ready to embrace life, I sometimes consider the "Law of Preparedness" **Matthew 22:14** "For many are called, but few *are* chosen."

When I lose focus on the good and become distracted from my purpose, the "**Laws of Attraction**" are indeed worth respecting. **Matthew 6:21** For where your treasure is, there your heart will be also.

When I am afraid to take risks, ask for help, change or grow, the "**Law of Supply**" is sometimes the secret to my transformation. **Matthew 7:7** [*Ask, Seek, Knock*] "**Ask** and it will be given to you; seek and you will find; knock and the door will be opened to you.

Favorite Author or Special Biographies

Biographies of Select Authors who have focused on: Human Potential, Self-Help, Inspiration, Personal Development, Self-Improvement, New Thought, Metaphysics, and Mind Sciences.

Wallace D. Wattles (1860-1911)

Wattles was an American author and success writer. His most famous work was *The Science of Getting Rich*, or otherwise known as: *Financial Success Through Creative Thought*. He did profess to study thinkers such as Descartes, Spinoza, Leibnitz, Schopenhauer, Hegel, and Emerson. Wattles has positively affected millions with his books and philosophy of Mind Sciences or New Thought. His other books, including *The Science of Being Great*, have some excellent commentary and mind exercises for metaphysical wholeness and health.

Dr. Charles F. Haanel (1866-1949)

Haanel wrote the *Master Key System* in the early 1900s, which sold over two-hundred-thousand copies by 1933. It originally had twenty-four parts. The book is devoted to mind development and achieving your life's dreams using applied metaphysics. Charles F. Haanel was an American author, millionaire, entrepreneur, and businessman who belonged to several Freemason-related societies: the American Scientific League, The Author's League of America, The American Society of Psychical Research, the St. Louis Humane Society, and the St. Louis Chamber of Commerce. *The Master Key System* is one of the classic studies in self-improvement, mind sciences, New Thought, and higher consciousness.

Robert Collier (1885– 1950)

Collier was an famous author of metaphysical books and self-improvement books in the twentieth century. Collier was born in St. Louis and was the nephew of the founder of *Collier's* magazine. He was involved in writing, editing, and research for most of his life. His book, *The Secret of the Ages*, sold over 300,000 copies during his life. Collier wrote about the practical psychology of abundance, desire, faith, visualization, confident action, and becoming your best. Robert Collier Publications, Inc., still exists through the efforts of his widow and now his children and grandchildren. Collier's books have recently been brought back to prominence from being referenced in the popular metaphysical movie, *The Secret*. Moreover, Robert Collier's books have been popular with self-help schools of thought and the Unity School of Christianity.

Prentice Mulford (1834-1891)

Prentice Mulford was an author, New Thought visionary, and adventurer. Born in Sag Harbor, Long Island, he sailed to San Francisco on a clipper in 1856 and remained for sixteen years. He left for a long tour of Europe in 1872 and then settled in New York City, where he became known as a comic lecturer and author of poems and essays and a columnist for the *New York Daily Graphic* (a serial), 1875-1881. He may have founded the popular philosophy known as New Thought.

Life by Land and Sea (1889) contains Mulford's adventures at sea and in the West (1856-1872), life on a clipper and a California coastal schooner hunting whales and seals, gold prospecting in Tuolumne County, accounts of camp life, and experiences as a school teacher and minor local politician, copper mining in Stanislaus County, and his career as journalist for the *San Francisco Golden Era*.

Dr. JOSEPH MURPHY, PHD, DRS, LL.D., (1898-1981)

Murphy lectured to hundreds of thousands of people all over the world for nearly fifty years on the powers of the subconscious mind and Spiritual abundance. Born in 1898, he was educated in Ireland and England. Years of research studying the world's major religions convinced him that some great Power lay behind them all: The Power is within you!

Dr. Murphy was Founder/Minister-Director of the Church of Religious/Divine Science in Los Angeles for twenty-eight years, where his lectures were attended by over a thousand people almost every Sunday. He wrote over thirty books, including *The Amazing Laws of Cosmic Mind, The Miracle of Mind Dynamics, Your Infinite Power to Be Rich, Secrets of the I-Ching,* and *The Cosmic Power Within You* and also the famous *The Power of Your Subconscious Mind.* It is claimed that Murphy was influenced by Troward and Fox.

Dr. Christian D. Larson

Larson was a famous New Thought leader and teacher as well as a prolific author of metaphysical and New Thought books in the early 1900s. Larson's writings affected many great teachers and founders of several religions and philosophies.

Larson was honorary president of the International New Thought Alliance. Moreover, he was a colleague of with such notables as W.W. Atkinson, Horatio Dresser, Charles Brodie Patterson, and Annie Rix Militz. Moreover, his teachings greatly affected the life of Religious Science founder, Ernest Holmes, in his early career. Holmes had been studying the Christian Science textbook but came upon the writings of Larson. According to sources he steered away his earlier loyalties toward Larson's teachings.

Jesus Christ - 0 BCE to 33 AD.

We reference Jesus Christ as his teachings and word have inspired most of the authors analyzed and discussed herein.

Buddha

Siddhārtha Gautama (Pali, Gotama Buddha) - a Spiritual teacher from ancient India who founded Buddhism. He is universally recognized by Buddhists as the Supreme Buddha. The time of his birth and death are approximately 563 BCE to 483 BCE, though some have suggested a later date.

The foundation of Buddhist philosophy may include: The Four Noble Truths: that suffering is an inherent part of existence, that the origin of suffering is ignorance and the main symptoms of that ignorance are attachment and craving, that attachment and craving can be ceased, and that following the Noble Eightfold Path will lead to the cessation of attachment and craving and therefore suffering.
The Noble Eightfold Path includes: right understanding, right thought, right speech, right action, right livelihood, right effort, right mindfulness, and right concentration.

Dr. Thomas Troward (1847-1916)

Troward authored many books that are considered classics in the area of New Thought, Mind Sciences, and even mystic Christianity. Influences on his writings include the teachings of Christ, Islam, Hindu Teachings, Buddhism, and more. Troward was born in Punjab, India, educated in England, and received honors in literature. Thomas Troward was appointed Her Majesty's Assistant Commissioner and later Divisional Judge of the North Indian Punjab from 1869 until his retirement in 1896. He was a prize-winning artist and loved to research and write. Troward was raised in the Church of England but was extremely well educated in the religions and philosophies of the world. Troward was the author of many successful books including the famous: *Edinburgh Lectures 1904* and *Dore Lectures*. Troward's writings have influenced many great authors and religious leaders such as: Emmet Fox, Ernest Holmes, Paul Foster Case, Joseph Murphy, and even recent authors such as Bob Proctor. His contributions to the development of the New Thought Movement, human potential research, and Religious Science continue in the present day. His writings are sometimes very intellectual, but his grasp on a fusion of Eastern and Western philosophy is intense and make for fruitful readings.

Because Troward did not see a need for the occult, his writings challenged dogma in favor of a personal and abundant relationship with the Universal Spirit similar to the philosophy of Pierre Teilhard de Chardin or other great recent mystics. Troward spoke several languages, studied biblical scripture written in Hebrew, read the Koran, and researched the writings of Raja Yoga. Several of his books are in the public domain due to their publication before the 1920's.

Dr. Napoleon Hill (1883–1970)

At a fairly young adult, Hill was commissioned by Andrew Carnegie, one of the most wealthy men in the world at the time, to produce a successful compilation of the best practices of millionaires. Hill interviewed many of the most wealthy and famous people alive at the time including Thomas Edison, Alexander Graham Bell, George Eastman, Henry Ford, Elmer Gates, William Jennings Bryan, Theodore Roosevelt, John D. Rockefeller, Charles M. Schwab, F.W. Woolworth, William Wrigley Jr., John Wanamaker, William H. Taft, Woodrow Wilson, Charles Allen Ward, and Jennings Randolph. The research and writing of *Think and Grow Rich* lasted over twenty years. Ultimately, Hill sold over thirty-million books. As for his personal influences, he did write a letter to Charles F. Haanel to say that Haanel's *Master Key System* had much inspired him and changed his life.

Throughout his life, he spent a great deal of time teaching and helping others to learn the laws of success.

Other great books by Napoleon Hill are *Think and Grow Rich* (ISBN 1-59330-200-2), *How to Sell Your Way through Life* (ISBN 0-910882-11-8), *The Law of Success* (ISBN 0-87980-447-5).
Success Through a Positive Mental Attitude (ISBN 1-55525-270-2), *You Can Work Your Own Miracles* (ISBN 0-449-91177-2), and *Napoleon Hill's Keys to Success* (ISBN 0-452-27281-5).

James Allen

Allen was born in Leicester, England in 1864. James was 15 when his father, **a** businessman, was murdered. He left school **to** work full time to help support the family. Eventually married and became an executive secretary for a large corporation. At age 38, he retired from employment and he and his wife moved to a small cottage on the southwest shore of England to pursue a simple life of contemplation. There he wrote for 9 years producing over 20 works. James Allen died in 1912 at age 48.

A philosophical writer of United Kingdom or British nationality. James Allen's books illustrate the power of thought to have immense capabilities. Allen never achieved great fame or wealth, his works continue to influence people around the world. Allen's most famous book, *As a Man Thinketh* was published in 1902.

Dr. William Walker Atkinson (1862-1932)

Atkinson wrote a multitude of books on New Thought by various names. He wrote nearly a hundred books with many other pseudonyms: Theodore Sheldon, Theron Q.Dumont, Swami Panchadasi, The Three Initiates, Magus Incognitus
Originally from Maryland, he married and later became interested in Mental Science and Hinduism. He was admitted to practice as a lawyer in Pennsylvania and Illinois. Around 1916, he began writing articles for Elizabeth Towne's magazine The Nautilus, and from 1916 to 1919 Atkinson edited the journal Advanced Thought, and for a time honorary president of the International New Thought Alliance.

Ralph Waldo Emerson (1803-1882)

Emerson is said to be the father of the American Renaissance. As he grew up in Boston, Emerson lived a difficult life with illness, poverty, and survived the death of his father when he was only 8 years old. His mother managed to raise 5 children alone, including one who was mentally challenged. At age 14, Emerson with the help of grants attended Harvard undergrad. After graduation, he taught at a girls school. Later, he returned to Harvard Divinity School. In 1829, after marrying Ellen Tucker, he was ordained a Unitarian minister. In 1831, his wife died, and he resigned from ministerial duties. He set off to Europe and Eurasia to seek and find himself. In 1835, having returned to the USA, Emerson married again to Lydia Jackson. In Concord, Massachusetts, they raised four children while Emerson gave Lectures and wrote poetry and prose combining his likes of philosophy and nature with politics. He was at the center of the American Transcendentalist movement. Emerson's major philosophy was that man and nature are the "essential perfectibility of the human spirit" and thought the ultimate meaning of life was the unity of the human soul with the divine oversoul. Emerson believed in "non conformity, creativeness, intellectual and spiritual independence, and self reliance." His contemporaries were among the likes of Henry Thoreau, Walt Whitman and Margaret Fuller. As a note, Emerson and William James did write essays and comment on Swedenborg. It seems that Swedenborg and Emerson did heavily influence the New Thought, Mind Science and other movements.

Edward Beals (?)

Beals wrote several books of which most are out of print. He wrote some books anonymously. X or Anonymous is sometimes the pen name for Edward Beals. He is said to have been a businessman with the spiritual gift of writing and editing who co-authored the Personal Power series with William W. Atkinson in the early 1920s. His anonymous book "The Laws of Success" is analyzed herein.

George Mentz, JD, MBA

Other References or Authors of Interest

Allen, J. (1998). *As You Think*. Ed. with introduction by M. Allen. Novato, CA: New World Library

Carnegie, D. (1994). *How to Win Friends and Influence People*. New York: Pocket Books. http://www.dalecarnegie.com

Carlson, R. (2001). *Don't Sweat the Small Stuff About Money*. Location: Hyperion. Previously published as *Don't Worry Make Money* http://www.dontsweat.com.

Chopra, D. (1996). *The Seven Spiritual Laws of Success*. London: Bantam Press. http://www.chopra.com

Collier, R. (1970). *Be Rich*. Oak Harbor, WA: Robert Collier Publishing. http://robertcollierpublications.com

Covey, S. R. (1989). *The 7 Habits of Highly Effective People*. London: Simon & Schuster. http://www.stephencovey.com

Dyer, W. (1993). *Real Magic: Creating Miracles in Everyday Life*. New York: HarperCollins. http://www.drwaynedyer.com

Gawain, Shakti (1979). *Creative Visualization*. Mill Valley: Publisher. http://www.shaktigawain.com

Haanel, Mentz (2006). *How to Master Abundance and Prosperity - The* Master Key System *Decoded*. Location: Xlibris Pub.

Carlson Haanel Wattles, Mentz (2005). *The Science of Growing Rich*. Location: Xlibris Publishing.

Hill, N. (1960). *Think and Grow Rich*, New York: Fawcett Crest.

His Holiness the Dalai Lama & Howard C. Cutler (1999). *The Art of Happiness: A handbook for Living*. London: Hodder & Stroughton. http://www.dalailama.com

James, William (1902).   *The Varieties of Religious Experience*. Location: Publisher.

Marden, O. S. (1997). *Pushing to the Front, or Success under Difficulties*, Vols 1 & 2. Santa Fe, CA: Sun Books.

Mentz, G. S. (2006) *Essays on New Thought and Success*. Location: LULU Publishing Corporation. http://www.lulu.com/gmentz

Mulford, Prentice (1908). *Thoughts are Things -
Essays Selected From The White Cross Library*. Location: Publisher.

Murphy, J. (2002). *The Power of Your Subconscious Mind*, New York: Bantam Books.

Ponder, C. (1962) *The Dynamic Laws of Prosperity*, Camarillo, CA: DeVorss & Co.

Roman & Packer (1988). *Creating Money*: Tiburon, CA: Kramer. http://www.orindaben.com

Price, J. R. (1987). *The Abundance Book*. Carlsbad, CA: Hay House. http://www.johnrandolphprice.com

Smiles, S. (2002). *Self-Help: With Illustrations of Character, Conduct, and Perseverance. Oxford, UK: Oxford University Press.*

Tracy, B. (1993). *Maximum Achievement: Strategies and Skills That Will Unlock Your Hidden Powers to Succeed.* New York: Fireside. http://www.briantracy.com

Troward, Judge Thomas (1904). *The Edinburgh Lectures on Mental Science.* Location: Publisher.

Wattles, W.D. (1976). *Financial Success through the Power of Thought* [*The Science of Getting Rich*]. Rochester, Vermont: Destiny Books. (Written originally around 1910).

Wilkinson, Bruce (2000). *The Prayer of Jabez.* City, OR: Multnamah Publishers. http://www.prayerofjabez.com

Prof. Dr. Mentz is the first person in the United States to be multi credentialed as a Lawyer, MBA, Licensed Wealth Manager, Certified Financial Consultant, and Licensed Financial Planner. Prof. Mentz has held faculty appointments with 10 Universities, Colleges and law schools globally and holds a Juris Doctorate in International Law and an MBA in International Business along with International Law Certificate/Diplomé. Mentz has training centers in over 10 countries, and his training companies have been quoted or featured in the Wall Street Journal, The Hindu National, Financial Times Asia, The Arab Times, The China Daily and El Norte Mexico. Mentz has published over 20 books and has taught over 110 college and graduate level courses.

Prof. Mentz has studied the greatest authors of personal growth and self help philosophy for over 20 years. He began researching metaphysics, human potential, Christian mystics, Eastern spirituality secret societies, ancient fraternal rites, and secret orders to extract the leading principles for growth of mind, body and soul. After reading some 500 books in the field of success and attending hundreds of lectures that discussed life improvement subjects, he has complied summaries of what he believes to be some of the most effective life strategies throughout the world. Mentz teaches a holistic view of wealth management using both practical and insightful methods.

Information and Other books by Dr. Mentz Include:

1) *How to Master Abundance And Prosperity...the Ancient Spiritual Keys to Success: The Master Key System Decoded & the Science of Getting Rich Unveiled* - Publisher: Xlibris Corporation (March 31, 2006) ISBN-10: 1425710352 ISBN-13: 978-1425710354

2) *The Science of Growing Rich in Life* - Publisher: Xlibris Corporation (December 30, 2005) - ISBN-10: 1599263165 ISBN-13: 978-1599263168

3) For more information, tools, free books and other information see: www.mastersofthesecrets.com or www.secretdecoded.com